John Burroughs

The Legality of Threat or Use of Nuclear Weapons

Recht und Zukunftsverantwortung

herausgegeben von

Prof. Dr. jur. Alexander Roßnagel
(Universität-Gesamthochschule Kassel)

Band 3

LIT

John Burroughs

The Legality of Threat or Use of Nuclear Weapons

A Guide to the Historic Opinion of the
International Court of Justice.

Foreword by

Phon van den Biesen
(International Association of Lawyers
against Nuclear Arms)

LIT

Die Deutsche Bibliothek – CIP-Einheitsaufnahme

Burroughs, John
The Legality of Threat or Use of Nuclear Weapons : A Guide to the Historic
Opinion of the International Court of Justice ; foreword by Phon van den Biesen /
John Burroughs . – Münster : LIT, 1997
 (Recht und Zukunftsverantwortung ; 3.)
 ISBN 3-8258-3516-2

NE: GT

© LIT VERLAG
 Dieckstr. 73 48145 Münster Tel. 0251–23 50 91 Fax 0251–23 19 72

Contents

Foreword ix

Preface and Acknowledgments xi

INTRODUCTION 1
   General illegality of the threat or use of nuclear weapons 1
   The obligation to eliminate nuclear weapons 2
   Implications 3

PART ONE – HISTORY AND PROCEDURE

   Chapter One: The Initiative to Seek an Advisory Opinion 9

   Chapter Two: Proceedings Before the Court 11

   Chapter Three: Lack of Jurisdiction Over the World Health
      Assembly Request 13

   Chapter Four: The Decision to Reply to the General
      Assembly Request 14

PART TWO – THE OPINION

   Chapter Five: The Unique Characteristics of Nuclear
      Weapons 19

   Chapter Six: Formal Legal Conclusions 21

   Chapter Seven: Absence of a Specific Authorization or
      Prohibition of the Threat or Use of Nuclear Weapons as Such 24
      The prohibitions of use of poisonous, chemical, and
         biological weapons 24
      The Nuclear Non-Proliferation Treaty and other agreements
         restricting possession and use 25
      General Assembly resolutions and the practice of non-use 26

   Chapter Eight: Constraints on Threat or Use of Nuclear Weapons
      Based on Human Rights, the Genocide Convention, and
      Environmental Law 28
         Human rights 28
         The prohibition of genocide 29
         Environmental law 29

Chapter Nine: General Illegality of Threat or Use of Nuclear
  Weapons Under Law Applicable in Armed Conflict 32
    Humanitarian law 32
    The law of neutrality 37

Chapter Ten: Constraints on Threat or Use of Nuclear
  Weapons Based on the United Nations Charter 38
    The United Nations Charter 38
    Necessity and proportionality 39
    Reprisals 40
    Threat and deterrence 41

Chapter Eleven: Uncertainty as to an Extreme Circumstance of
  Self-Defense in Which the Very Survival of a State Is at Stake 44

Chapter Twelve: The Obligation to Bring to a Conclusion
  Negotiations on Nuclear Disarmament in All Its Aspects 48

PART THREE – THE JUDGES' SEPARATE STATEMENTS

Chapter Thirteen: The Judges' Individual Views on General
  Illegality, the Extreme Circumstance/Survival of the State
  Provision, and Nuclear Disarmament 55

CONCLUSION 66

Endnotes 70

APPENDIX A – STATES' ARGUMENTS TO THE COURT

Introduction 84

The Effects of Nuclear Weapons 88

Humanitarian Law 95
  Indiscriminate harm and unnecessary suffering 97
  General principles of humanity and the Martens Clause 99

Environmental Law 103
  The prohibition of causing severe damage to the
    environment 103
  General environmental law 105

Reprisals 107

The Law of Neutrality 110

Human Rights 111

The Prohibition of Poisonous and Analogous Weapons 114

The Prohibition of Genocide 116

General Assembly Resolutions and the Nuclear
    Non-Proliferation Treaty 117
        General Assembly resolutions 117
        The Nuclear Non-Proliferation Treaty, regional nuclear
            weapon free zones, and other agreements and
            commitments 119
The United Nations Charter 127
Threat and Deterrence 132
Endnotes to Appendix A 145

APPENDIX B – States' Responses to the Opinion 151

APPENDIX C – World Health Assembly Resolution WHA46.40,
    Adopted 14 May 1993, Requesting Advisory Opinion 157

APPENDIX D – General Assembly Resolution 49/75 K, Adopted
    15 December 1994, Requesting Advisory Opinion 159

APPENDIX E – General Assembly Resolution 51/45 M, Adopted
    10 December 1996, Calling for Compliance with Advisory
    Opinion by Commencement of Negotiations Leading Toward
    a Nuclear Weapons Convention 161

Further Reading 163

Contacts 167

Contributors 169

Foreword

On 8 July 1996, the International Court of Justice decisively changed the global debate on nuclear weapons.

In its Advisory Opinion on the Legality of the Threat or Use of Nuclear Weapons, the World Court explained that the threat or use of nuclear weapons *would generally be contrary to the rules of international law applicable in armed conflict.* The Court found that the use of nuclear weapons "seems scarcely reconcilable" with the requirements of humanitarian law protecting civilians and combatants from unnecessary and indiscriminate effects of warfare, and further found that the nuclear weapon states had not demonstrated any circumstances justifying legal use. While the Court could not "conclude definitively whether the threat or use of nuclear weapons would be lawful or unlawful in an extreme circumstance of self-defence, in which the very survival of a State would be at stake," it also concluded that any threat or use of nuclear weapons should be in conformity with humanitarian law. Thus the Court placed an impossible burden of proof on the nuclear weapon states to justify any nuclear threat or use.

It is clear that this Opinion, which clarifies the precise meaning of binding rules of international law, in particular of the rules of humanitarian law, should lead the nuclear weapon states to an early review of their nuclear weapon policies. Indeed, it should move the entire world community into action designed to start the next century free of the curse of nuclear weapons. Without being asked to do so, the Court also gave its advice on the meaning of Article VI of the Nuclear Non-Proliferation Treaty, which provision calls for good faith negotiations towards nuclear disarmament. The Court unanimously concluded that this is not just a vague policy statement, but a legal obligation to achieve a precise result. The obligation is not only to negotiate, but also to *bring to a conclusion negotiations leading to nuclear disarmament in all its aspects under strict and effective international control.*

The importance of this section of the Advisory Opinion cannot be overstated. It means that states which are at this very moment *not* involved in a negotiating process specifically focused on the goal of total nuclear disarmament, are at this very moment violating their obligations under international law. The natural outcome of such a negotiating process would be the adoption of a comprehensive Nuclear Weapons Convention creating a framework for the complete elimination of nuclear weapons.

In addition to this call for action there is a great deal to be learned from this Advisory Opinion, not only for lawyers and lawyers-to-be, but also for policy-makers, parliamentarians, and activists. The Opinion makes it clear that the law indeed provides a normative standard for civilized behavior. It confirms that big powers cannot dictate or define the law as a function of power politics; rather they too are bound and restricted by law, including principles of international law derived from established custom, from the principles of humanity, and from the dictates of the public conscience. The Opinion, furthermore, shows that the International Court of Justice is on its way to becoming *the* independent adjudicator of justice, one of the building blocks for a truly civilized world.

The Opinion also shows how legal arguments can be added effectively to a struggle in which moral, religious, ideological, military and political arguments have been predominant.

It demonstrates that a worldwide citizens' movement is able to get governments moving, since it was this movement that encouraged and convinced a majority of states to bring the nuclear weapons issue before the International Court of Justice.

In providing its important answers to the question asked by the General Assembly of the United Nations, the Court also produced a wealth of material on the laws of war, including significant observations on the relevance of human rights and environmental law, which will be scrutinized and debated for many years to come. In this respect the separate or dissenting opinions added by each of the individual judges of the Court are of great value to the further development of international law.

This book opens the door to the Advisory Opinion, for lawyers and non-lawyers alike. It also opens the door to the legal, and sometimes political, arguments put before the Court by the many states who participated in the Court proceedings.

This book is meant as an explanation and celebration of the most authoritative legal findings the world has available on the nuclear weapons issue: the Advisory Opinion of the International Court of Justice of 8 July 1996.

Phon van den Biesen
International Association of Lawyers Against Nuclear Arms
Amsterdam
19 September 1997

Preface and Acknowledgments

The International Association of Lawyers Against Nuclear Arms (IALANA) played a principal role in bringing the question of the legality of nuclear weapons before the International Court of Justice, along with the International Physicians for the Prevention of Nuclear War and the International Peace Bureau. In 1992, the three organizations together launched the World Court Project, which was eventually endorsed by over 700 organizations worldwide. IALANA lawyers subsequently drafted model briefs and consulted with several states concerning their oral arguments before the Court at the November 1995 hearings.

Drawing on this experience, IALANA intends this book to be a guide to the Court's conclusions, its underlying legal analysis, and the separate statements of the judges. The book also explains the implications of the Advisory Opinion – above all, abandonment of reliance on the threat of nuclear weapons as an instrument of national policy and expeditious achievement of nuclear disarmament.

The significance of the case, however, lies not only in the Opinion. The process of obtaining the Opinion was itself extraordinary. As the book recounts, the initiative to put the question before the Court involved millions of people around the world and a close working relationship between the World Court Project and states that for decades have condemned nuclear weapons in the United Nations General Assembly. Then, in the written and oral proceedings that preceded issuance of the opinion, states arguing for illegality made brilliant, eloquent, and moving presentations, regarding both the legal issues and the effects of nuclear weapons when used on Hiroshima and Nagasaki and tested in the Pacific. In many ways, states illuminated important aspects of the problem that were only touched upon by the Court. Appendix A describes states' presentations, quoting extensively from their arguments to the Court, and is recommended to the reader seeking a deeper understanding of the issues.

The World Court Project/IALANA legal team at the November 1995 hearings, in addition to the author, comprised Peter Weiss, co-president of IALANA and president of the Lawyers' Committee on Nuclear Policy (LCNP), the U.S. affiliate of IALANA; Phon van den Biesen, secretary of IALANA; Alyn Ware, executive director of LCNP; and Anabel Dwyer, member of the board of directors of LCNP. Each made extensive comments on earlier versions and other significant contributions to this book. Anabel Dwyer played a critical role in getting the book underway, assembling and synthesizing materials and preparing an initial draft. Parts of the book draw on articles by Peter Weiss.

Others who made helpful contributions include Jacqueline Cabasso, executive director of the Western States Legal Foundation, David Krieger, president of the Nuclear Age Peace Foundation, and Robert Green and Kate Dewes of World Court Project UK and World Court Project Aotearoa.

In a larger sense, this book reflects the efforts of lawyers, physicians, politicians, diplomats, and activists, of whom only a few could be mentioned in the following pages, who have worked for years and in some cases decades to subject nuclear weapons to the rule of law.

John Burroughs
Western States Legal Foundation
Oakland, California
22 September 1997

Introduction

In an historic opinion issued 8 July 1996, the International Court of Justice (ICJ) held that the threat or use of nuclear weapons is generally illegal, and that states are obligated to bring to a conclusion negotiations on nuclear disarmament in all its aspects.[1] Popularly known as the World Court, the ICJ is the judicial branch of the United Nations, and the highest and most authoritative court in the world on questions of international law. Its statement of the law governing nuclear weapons is therefore of signal importance.

General illegality of the threat or use of nuclear weapons
In a formal conclusion, the Court held that "*the threat or use of nuclear weapons would generally be contrary to the rules of international law applicable in armed conflict, and in particular the principles and rules of humanitarian law.*"[2] This conclusion is powerfully supported by key elements of the Court's analysis, including:
• Nuclear weapons have "unique characteristics," including "their destructive capacity, their capacity to cause untold human suffering, and their ability to cause damage to generations to come;" their "destructive power ... cannot be contained in either space or time;" a nuclear explosion "releases not only immense quantities of heat and energy, but also powerful and prolonged radiation," which "would affect health, agriculture, natural resources and demography over a very wide area," and "has the potential to damage the future environment, food and marine ecosystem, and to cause genetic defects and illness in future generations;"[3]
• Under humanitarian law, "methods and means of warfare, which would preclude any distinction between civilian and military targets, or which would result in unnecessary suffering to combatants, are prohibited. In view of the unique characteristics of nuclear weapons, ... the use of such weapons in fact seems scarcely reconcilable with respect for such requirements;"[4]
• Self-defence warrants "only measures which are proportional to the armed attack and necessary to respond to it," and "a use of force that is proportionate under the law of self-defence, must, in order to be lawful, also

meet the requirements of the law applicable in armed conflict which comprise in particular the principles and rules of humanitarian law;"[5]

• The environment "represents the living space, the quality of life and the very health of human beings, including generations unborn," and "States must take environmental considerations into account when assessing what is necessary and proportionate in the pursuit of legitimate military objectives" and in implementation of the law applicable in armed conflict;[6]

• The nuclear weapon states failed to demonstrate that any use of nuclear weapons, including a "clean" use involving "low yield" weapons, could comply with legal requirements or avoid catastrophic escalation;[7]

• "[I]f the use of force itself in a given case is illegal – for whatever reason – the threat to use such force will likewise be illegal."[8]

The force of the holding that threat or use is generally illegal is thus overwhelming when viewed in the context of the entire opinion. It was qualified by the statement that "the Court cannot conclude definitely whether the threat or use of nuclear weapons would be lawful or unlawful in an extreme circumstance of self-defence, in which the very survival of a State would be at stake."[9] In explanation, the Court referred to the right of self-defence, the policy of deterrence, whose legality the Court declined directly to assess, and the elements of fact and law at its disposal. However, threat or use in such a circumstance remains subject to the requirements of humanitarian law. As the Court stated, a *"fundamental"* and *"intransgressible"* rule is that "States must *never* make civilians the object of attack and must consequently *never* use weapons that are incapable of distinguishing between civilian and military targets."[10]

The strength of the general illegality conclusion is further revealed by the voting pattern. Both that conclusion and the extreme circumstance/survival of the state provision are set forth in paragraph 2E of the dispositif, which records the Court's formal conclusions. The entire paragraph was voted for by seven of the fourteen judges then serving on the Court, and was adopted as the Court's opinion based on the casting vote of the President, Mohammed Bedjaoui. But, the judges' separate statements show that while the extreme circumstance/survival of the state provision was intensely controversial, support for general or categorical illegality was broad and deep. Three judges declined to vote for paragraph 2E because it did not definitively hold threat or use of nuclear weapons to be categorically illegal, that is, illegal in every circumstance. Thus ten judges supported at least a holding of general illegality.

The obligation to eliminate nuclear weapons

In paragraph 2F of the dispositif, the Court unanimously held that *"[t]here exists an obligation to pursue in good faith and bring to a conclusion negotiations leading to nuclear disarmament in all its aspects under strict and effective international control."* The Court explained that Article

VI of the Nuclear Non-Proliferation Treaty (NPT) imposes "an obligation to achieve a precise result – nuclear disarmament in all its aspects – by adopting a particular course of conduct, namely, the pursuit of negotiations on the matter in good faith."[11] The Court observed that 182 states, "the vast majority of the international community," are parties to the NPT, and that nuclear disarmament is "an objective of vital importance to the whole of the international community today."[12]

Endorsed by every judge on the Court, this is now the authoritative interpretation of Article VI of the NPT, and is perhaps the most important result of the case. Its importance is underlined by the fact that it was not required by the request of the General Assembly of the United Nations for clarification of the legal status of threat or use of nuclear weapons, but rather was produced on the Court's own initiative. In the Court's view, elimination of nuclear weapons is the only adequate response to the dilemmas and risks posed by the nuclear age. Of special significance is the holding that Article VI requires states to *achieve* nuclear disarmament through good faith negotiation. Talking is not enough; the talk must lead to action. Also important is that the Court delinked the obligation to achieve nuclear disarmament from the obligation, also found in Article VI, to establish a treaty on general and complete disarmament. Nuclear weapon states can no longer plausibly rely on the rationale that elimination of nuclear weapons must await comprehensive global disarmament. Also significant is the implication that the obligation applies to all states, not only those who are party to the NPT, thus binding such threshold states as India, Israel, and Pakistan.

Implications

The Court's holdings came in response to a request for an advisory opinion by the General Assembly, not in the context of a contentious case that concerns a specific dispute among states. Because it is advisory, the opinion as such is not directly binding on the United Nations or its member states. However, the ICJ has authoritatively interpreted law which states acknowledge they must follow, including humanitarian law, the United Nations Charter, and Article VI of the NPT. Accordingly, the opinion is binding in the sense that states must comply with the law it applies. It can be cited as an authoritative statement of the law in any political or legal setting – including NPT review conferences, the General Assembly, national courts or parliaments, or the ICJ itself – in which nuclear weapon policies are challenged.

While noting the opinion's advisory character, the nuclear weapon states have not sought to deny its authority. Rather they have claimed that their policies comply with the law as stated in the opinion, referring to the Court's refusal directly to pass upon deterrence, its uncertainty with respect to an extreme circumstance of self-defence in which the very survival of a state is at stake, and arms control and non-proliferation measures such as United States-Russian bilateral reductions and the Comprehensive Test Ban Treaty.[13]

Most of the world disagrees. One hundred fifteen states voted for the December 1996 General Assembly resolution initiated by Malaysia calling for compliance with the opinion by commencement in 1997 of negotiations leading towards a nuclear weapons convention.[14] To show that this is workable, the International Association of Lawyers Against Nuclear Arms, its U.S. affiliate, the Lawyers' Committee on Nuclear Policy, the International Network of Engineers and Scientists Against Proliferation, and others have drafted a model nuclear weapons convention. Like the chemical and biological weapons conventions already in force, the model convention sets forth an institutional framework and measures accomplishing the total abolition of nuclear weapons. Numerous states have also demanded nuclear disarmament in compliance with the opinion in proceedings reviewing implementation of the NPT.

Other developments are also promising. Abolition 2000: A Global Network to Eliminate Nuclear Weapons, was formed at the November 1995 hearings on the nuclear weapons case before the ICJ in The Hague and now comprises more than 700 groups worldwide. The Network has made conclusion of a nuclear weapons convention its central demand. The Canadian Abolition 2000 Network, led by former Canadian Ambassador for Disarmament Douglas Roche, conducted a series of town meetings discussing Canada's policy in light of the opinion. The conclusions of the process, in particular that Canada should work for an end to NATO's reliance on nuclear weapons, were presented at a parliamentary hearing. World Court Project activists in the United Kingdom similarly have engaged policymakers in dialogue about the implications of the case, as have activists in other countries. Numerous cities have passed resolutions calling for creation of a nuclear weapon free world in compliance with the opinion. Non-violent direct action campaigns have demanded the withdrawal of nuclear weapons from deployment based on the opinion, and it has been cited in defending against prosecutions arising out of protest actions.[15]

As these initiatives reflect, contrary to the claims of the nuclear weapon states, deterrence policies are highly vulnerable to challenge in light of the opinion. While the Court declined to confront deterrence head on, it did hold that that a threat of use of illegal force is itself illegal. In realistic scenarios, no type of nuclear weapon now deployed can be used or threatened to be used in compliance with humanitarian and other applicable law. As a committee of the U.S. National Academy of Sciences stated:

> [T]he ICJ unanimously agreed that the threat or use of nuclear weapons is strictly limited by generally accepted laws and humanitarian principles that restrict the use of force.

Accordingly, any threat or use of nuclear weapons must be limited to, and necessary for, self defense; it must not be targeted at civilians, and be capable of distinguishing between civilian and military targets; and it must not cause unnecessary suffering to combatants, or harm greater than that unavoidable to achieve military objectives. In the committee's view, *the inherent destructiveness of nuclear weapons, combined with the unavoidable risk that even the most restricted use of such weapons would escalate to broader attacks, makes it extremely unlikely that any contemplated threat or use of nuclear weapons would meet these criteria.*[16]

Moreover, the illegal threat of use is inherent in the postures of deterrence (hair trigger deployment, declared policies of massive retaliation, first use, and defence of "vital interests," etc.) now continuously maintained by the nuclear weapon states absent any extreme circumstance of self-defence in which their very survival is at stake.[17] Such postures are also inconsistent with implementation of the obligation to eliminate nuclear arsenals through good faith negotiation.

The opinion therefore mandates the immediate implementation of measures to reduce the level of threat and risk in existing nuclear postures like those recommended by the U.S. National Academy of Sciences and the Canberra Commission on the Elimination of Nuclear Weapons.[18] These include adoption of unconditional no first use commitments, taking nuclear forces off alert, and separation of warheads from delivery systems. And, consistent with the calls for the abolition of nuclear weapons now being made by these and other authorities, most states, and citizens' groups around the world, the Court unanimously recognized that the only viable permanent response to the illegality of threat or use is the achievement, in compliance with the NPT, of nuclear disarmament in all its aspects.

PART ONE

HISTORY AND PROCEDURE

♦ Chapter One ♦

The Initiative to Seek an Advisory Opinion

In 1993, despite the determined opposition of the nuclear weapon states, non-nuclear countries mustered a comfortable majority in the World Health Assembly, the governing body of the World Health Organization (WHO), a United Nations agency, to request an advisory opinion on the following question: "In view of the health and environmental effects, would the use of nuclear weapons by a State in war or other armed conflict be a breach of its obligations under international law including the WHO Constitution?"[19] The request was based on a longstanding WHO concern with issues relating to radioactivity, in particular two reports WHO published in the 1980s regarding the effects of nuclear war on health and health services.[20]

In 1994, the United Nations General Assembly followed suit, passing a resolution that posed the broader question: "Is the threat or use of nuclear weapons in any circumstance permitted under international law?"[21] In 1993, the same resolution had been defeated due to intense lobbying by the nuclear weapon states. Active support from anti-nuclear weapon groups around the world helped ensure its success in 1994. The General Assembly request was intended in part to overcome objections to the standing of the WHO in raising a question involving issues of peace and security.

A coalition of civic organizations (sometimes referred to as non-governmental organizations or "NGOs")[22] known as the World Court Project was instrumental in persuading the WHO and the General Assembly to make the requests. The World Court Project was launched in 1992 by the International Association of Lawyers Against Nuclear Arms (IALANA), the International Physicians for the Prevention of Nuclear War (IPPNW), and the International Peace Bureau (IPB). More than 700 groups from countries around the world endorsed the World Court Project. Many lent their support by asking their governments to vote for the WHO and General Assembly requests. The World Court Project also lobbied intensively at the WHO in Geneva and the General Assembly in New York, working closely with Non-Aligned Movement states that for decades had condemned nuclear weapons in General Assembly resolutions.

The World Court Project built on earlier work. In 1985, the London Nuclear Warfare Tribunal was convened by IPB and other groups. The Tribunal was chaired by Sean MacBride, IPB president and former Irish Foreign Minister, and included Richard Falk, professor of international law at Princeton University and long-time scholar of the legal framework for nuclear weapons policy.[23] The Tribunal declared the threat or use of nuclear weapons to be illegal, and recommended "the initiation of an effort to obtain an Advisory Opinion of the International Court of Justice on the status of nuclear weapons, strategic doctrines and war plans."[24]

In 1987, Aotearoa/New Zealand retired judge Harold Evans commenced a letter writing campaign to persuade governments to seek an advisory opinion.[25] In 1988 IPPNW endorsed the initiative, as did IPB in 1989. Both organizations are Nobel Peace Prize winners. IPPNW subsequently was the key actor convincing WHO member states to request an opinion from the ICJ.[26] In 1987, the U.S.-based Lawyers' Committee on Nuclear Policy, an advocate of resort to the ICJ since its inception in 1982, and Soviet lawyers held a conference in New York which led to the formation of IALANA. In 1989, IALANA adopted the Hague Declaration condemning nuclear weapons as illegal and backed the ICJ initiative.

In 1992, Keith Mothersson, a co-founder of World Court Project-UK, created a "declaration of public conscience" opposing nuclear weapons as immoral and illegal.[27] The declaration was inspired by a provision contained in the Hague and Geneva treaties known as the Martens Clause in honor of its author, Russian foreign minister Feodoro de Martens. The Martens Clause identifies "dictates of the public conscience" as a factor in determining whether a means of warfare not expressly addressed by treaty is nonetheless prohibited or regulated by international law. Individual declarations eventually were signed by nearly four million persons worldwide, the large majority from Japan, and presented to the registrar of the Court, a first in the Court's history.

IALANA lawyers drafted model briefs that many non-nuclear weapon countries used in making written submissions to the court. The principal IALANA brief was authored by Peter Weiss, Burns Weston, Richard Falk, and Saul Mendlovitz.[28] Other IALANA lawyers making contributions to the model briefs included Phon van den Biesen, Merav Datan, and Michael Bothe. At the November 1995 hearings, IALANA/World Court Project lawyers and activists consulted with several non-nuclear weapon states concerning their presentations, and staffed an information clearinghouse, preparing daily updates for distribution internationally to supporters and the press.

♦ Chapter Two ♦

Proceedings Before the Court

Article 92 of the United Nations Charter establishes the International Court of Justice as the principal judicial organ of the United Nations. The Statute of the International Court of Justice annexed to the Charter further specifies the ICJ's functions. The ICJ hears two types of cases, contentious and advisory. Contentious cases involve disputes among two or more states. In such a case states are obligated to respect the Court's judgment, which can be enforced through the Security Council.[29] Advisory opinions are intended to provide U.N. bodies guidance regarding legal issues, and are not directly binding on the U.N. or its member states or enforceable as such. However, as Judge Shahabuddeen has observed, "… although an advisory opinion has no binding force under article 59 of the Statute, it is as authoritative a statement of the law as a judgment rendered in contentious proceedings."[30]

The Court sits at the International Peace Palace in The Hague, Netherlands. It is normally composed of 15 judges, but 14 judges heard the nuclear weapons cases due to the death of Judge Andres Aguilar Mawdsley of Venezuela shortly before the hearings. When there is an even number of judges, in the event of a tie the President of the Court casts the deciding vote. Each judge must be from a different country, and the judges must represent the various legal systems and regions of the world. By custom, the ICJ includes representatives from each of the permanent five members of the Security Council (France, China, United Kingdom, Russia, and United States). The 14 judges, and their states of citizenship, were:

- President Mohammed Bedjaoui (Algeria)
- Vice-President Stephen M. Schwebel (United States)
- Shigeru Oda (Japan)
- Gilbert Guillaume (France)
- Mohamed Shahabuddeen (Guyana)
- Christopher G. Weeramantry (Sri Lanka)
- Raymond Ranjeva (Madagascar)
- Géza Herczegh (Hungary)
- Shi Jiuyong (China)
- Carl-August Fleischhauer (Germany)
- Abdul G. Koroma (Sierra Leone)

- Vladlen S. Vereshchetin (Russian Federation)
- Liugi Ferrari Bravo (Italy)
- Rosalyn Higgins (United Kingdom)

States could participate in the WHO and General Assembly cases by making written submissions, by making oral presentations during two weeks of hearings held in November 1995, or both. Twenty-two states argued at the hearings, of which all but two (Indonesia and Zimbabwe) also made written submissions. Another 23 states made written submissions only. All told, 45 states and the WHO participated, by far the largest total in the Court's history. Leading Non-Aligned Movement states like Egypt, Mexico, and Malaysia made strong showings, as did other states like New Zealand and Australia. Despite their small size, three Pacific Island states, Samoa, the Marshall Islands, and the Solomon Islands, made substantial contributions. Of the declared nuclear weapon states, only China did not participate. However, China has often stated in other forums its commitment to unconditional no first use and early conclusion of an abolition convention. Of the undeclared ("threshold") nuclear weapon states, India made written arguments for illegality; Pakistan and Israel did not participate.

Oral argument before the Court was dramatic – intense, eloquent, and well framed and conceived. In both the written and oral proceedings, states brilliantly mapped out the issues that were addressed by the Court. Indeed, in many respects the states illuminated important aspects of the problem that were only touched upon by the Court. More than two-thirds of the participating states contended that nuclear weapons are instruments of mass destruction whose effects are inherently indiscriminate, inhumane, and uncontrollable, and whose use is therefore illegal. The nuclear weapon states, along with certain NATO states, countered that there is no treaty expressly banning use of nuclear weapons comparable to conventions on chemical and biological weapons. Whether use is legal, they asserted, depends on the circumstances of each case and cannot be prejudged. (For a detailed account of states' arguments, see Appendix A.)

The states making oral arguments were Australia, Costa Rica, Egypt, France, Germany, Indonesia, Iran, Italy, Japan, Malaysia, the Marshall Islands, Mexico, New Zealand, the Philippines, Qatar, the Russian Republic, Samoa, San Marino, the Solomon Islands, the United Kingdom, the United States, and Zimbabwe.

The states making written submissions only were Azerbaijan, Bosnia and Herzegovina, Burundi, Colombia, Democratic People's Republic of Korea, Ecuador, Finland, India, Ireland, Kazakhstan, Lesotho, Lithuania, Moldova, Nauru, Netherlands, Norway, Papua New Guinea, Rwanda, Saudi Arabia, Sri Lanka, Sweden, Uganda, and Ukraine.

♦ Chapter Three ♦

Lack of Jurisdiction Over the World Health Assembly Request

States' oral arguments to the Court largely concerned the General Assembly question. That question was broader in scope than the WHO question, and did not raise similar issues of whether the WHO had standing to bring the legality of nuclear weapons before the Court. Nonetheless, certain states argued vigorously that the Court should decide the WHO question. Notably, it was urged that WHO had every right to be concerned with the legality of nuclear weapons as an aspect of a health centered mission of preventing nuclear war. The WHO had found that prevention of such a war is the only realistic medical response. In a cursory opinion, the ICJ found that by the terms of its Constitution, the WHO had no competence in the matter of the legality, as opposed to the effects, of the use of nuclear weapons.[31]

The WHO, the Court noted, had been authorized by the General Assembly to request advisory opinions on "legal questions arising within the scope of its competence."[32] However, according to the Court, "the legality or illegality of the use of nuclear weapons in no way determines the specific measures, regarding health or otherwise (studies, plans, procedures, etc.) which could be necessary in order to seek to prevent or cure some of their effects."[33] Judges Shahabuddeen, Weeramantry, and Koroma dissented. Weeramantry stated, "The impossibility of curative steps forces WHO into the area of prevention."[34]

Notwithstanding the ICJ's refusal to decide the WHO question, the WHO initiative was of great importance. It paved the way for the General Assembly request. It also put squarely before the Court the major WHO studies of the effects of nuclear war on health and health services, studies upon which the Court clearly relied in its finding regarding the "unique characteristics" of nuclear weapons in the opinion responding to the General Assembly request.

♦ Chapter Four ♦

The Decision to Reply to the General Assembly Request

The Court had no difficulty in holding that it had the authority to reply to the General Assembly request. The U.N. Charter provides that the General Assembly may seek an advisory opinion on "any legal question," without stating any limitations.[35] The Court observed that the request clearly posed legal issues relating to whether the threat or use of nuclear weapons is compatible with international law. Even if the Charter is interpreted to limit the General Assembly to asking questions within the scope of its activities (a matter the Court did not decide), it engages in many activities, such as resolutions, studies, debates, and special sessions, relating to disarmament and international security. Moreover, the fact that a question has political motives, aspects, or consequences is of no moment so long as it has a legal character. The Court noted that "in situations in which political considerations are prominent it may be particularly necessary for an international organization to obtain an advisory opinion from the Court as to the legal principles applicable with respect to the matter under debate."[36]

The nuclear weapon states and NATO states had, however, implored the ICJ to exercise its discretion to decline to respond to the request. They argued that the court should refrain from issuing an opinion on the legality of nuclear weapons because the question is too abstract and hypothetical for judicial analysis. France stated that the Court has been "placed in the position of a mathematician asked to solve an equation containing an infinite number of unknowns."[37] They also argued that the General Assembly had no clear purpose for asking the question, that a response might adversely affect ongoing negotiations, and that the question required the Court to legislate rather than interpret existing law.

The non-nuclear weapon countries argued that it is the duty of the court, as a U.N. organ, to respond to the General Assembly. No speculation about the effects of nuclear explosions is required, they contended, after Hiroshima and Nagasaki, the experience of test site downwinders, and the WHO studies of the health consequences of nuclear war. "To postpone giving a legal opinion on the threat or use of nuclear weapons until an actual case occurs is like substituting medicine with an autopsy," stated Mexico.[38]

The Court noted that while it does have discretion to decline to respond to a request for an advisory opinion, previous cases established that it should do so only based on "compelling" reasons. No such compelling reasons had been advanced, the Court found, with only Judge Oda dissenting, and it therefore would provide the opinion. In previous cases, it was made clear that the abstractness of a legal question, or its lack of relation to a specific dispute, were not reasons to refuse to provide requested legal guidance. Further,

> The Court does not consider that, in giving an advisory opinion in the present case, it would necessarily have to write "scenarios," to study various types of nuclear weapons and to evaluate highly complex and controversial technological, strategic and scientific information. The Court will simply address the issues arising in all their aspects by applying the legal rules relevant to the situation.[39]

As for the General Assembly's purposes in seeking an opinion, it "has the right to decide for itself on the usefulness of an opinion in the light of its own needs."[40] Concerning ongoing disarmament negotiations, the effect of an opinion "is a matter of appreciation," *i.e.* cannot be objectively determined, and is therefore irrelevant in deciding whether to respond.[41] Finally, the Court "states the existing law and does not legislate. This is so even if, in stating and applying the law, the Court necessarily has to specify its scope and sometimes note its general trend."[42]

PART TWO

THE OPINION

♦ Chapter Five ♦

The Unique Characteristics of Nuclear Weapons

In any case, before any court, there are two critical components: the facts at issue, and the applicable law. It is therefore of great significance that the ICJ's factual findings were very strong, virtually compelling the Court's conclusion that use of nuclear weapons is generally illegal, and indeed further implying that existing types of nuclear weapons cannot lawfully used be in *any* circumstance.

Powerful evidence about the effects of nuclear weapons from the 1984 and 1987 reports of the World Health Organization[43] and other authoritative sources was before the Court. While refraining from expressing an opinion as to how the Court should respond to the WHO request, the WHO's legal counsel noted that the WHO 1984 report "envisaged three possible scenarios: the use of a single bomb, a limited war and a total war. The number of dead in each of these scenarios varied from one million to one thousand million, to which the same number of people injured was to be added."[44]

The Solomon Islands submitted a declaration by Joseph Rotblat, radiation physicist and biologist, rapporteur for the WHO studies, former Manhattan Project physicist, and the 1995 Nobel Peace Prize winner. Rotblat stated that in addition to the initial blast, heat, and radiation effects of nuclear war, the long-term radiation effects would be global in scope, increasing the incidence of cancer and genetic defects. Japan presented Takashi Hiraoka, mayor of Hiroshima, and Iccho Ito, mayor of Nagasaki, to testify about their cities' horrific experiences. The Marshall Islands introduced Lijon Eknilang of the Rongelap Atoll local government. She described the effects of her community's exposure to radiation from a United States atmospheric test explosion, including the birth of "jellyfish" babies with no bones and transparent skin. (For more regarding these presentations, see "Effects of Nuclear Weapons," Appendix A.)

While the United States objected that the World Health Organization's "assumptions" in its reports were "highly selective,"[45] the nuclear weapon states did not make any significant effort to rebut the evidence submitted in support of the anti-nuclear case, and the Court accepted the thrust of that evidence in its factual findings:

[N]uclear weapons are explosive devices whose energy results from the fusion or fission of the atom. By its very nature, that process, in nuclear weapons as they exist today, releases not only immense quantities of heat and energy, but also powerful and prolonged radiation. According to the material before the Court, the first two causes of damage are vastly more powerful than the damage caused by other weapons, while the phenomenon of radiation is said to be peculiar to nuclear weapons. These characteristics render the nuclear weapon potentially catastrophic. The destructive power of nuclear weapons cannot be contained in either space or time. They have the potential to destroy all civilization and the entire ecosystem of the planet.

The radiation released by a nuclear explosion would affect health, agriculture, natural resources and demography over a very wide area. Further, the use of nuclear weapons would be a serious danger to future generations. Ionizing radiation has the potential to damage the future environment, food and marine ecosystem, and to cause genetic defects and illness in future generations.

In consequence, in order correctly to apply to the present case the Charter law on the use of force and the law applicable in armed conflict, in particular humanitarian law, it is imperative for the Court to take account of the unique characteristics of nuclear weapons, and in particular their destructive capacity, their capacity to cause untold human suffering, and their ability to cause damage to generations to come.[46]

♦ Chapter Six ♦

Formal Legal Conclusions

The Court's formal legal conclusions, set forth in the final paragraph and known as the dispositif,[47] were as follows:

A. Unanimously,

> There is in neither customary nor conventional international law any specific authorization of the threat or use of nuclear weapons;

B. By eleven votes to three,

> There is in neither customary nor conventional international law any comprehensive and universal prohibition of the threat or use of nuclear weapons as such;

> In Favour: President Bedjaoui; Vice-President Schwebel; Judges Oda, Guillaume, Ranjeva, Herczegh, Shi, Fleischhauer, Vereshchetin, Ferrari Bravo, Higgins;

> Against: Judges Shahabuddeen, Weeramantry, Koroma.

C. Unanimously,

> A threat or use of force by means of nuclear weapons that is contrary to Article 2, paragraph 4, of the United Nations Charter and that fails to meet all the requirements of Article 51, is unlawful;

D. Unanimously,

> A threat or use of nuclear weapons should also be compatible with the requirements of the international law applicable in armed conflict, particularly those of the principles and rules of international humanitarian law, as well as with specific obligations under treaties and other undertakings which expressly deal with nuclear weapons;

E. By seven votes to seven, by the President's casting vote,

> It follows from the above-mentioned requirements that the threat or use of nuclear weapons would generally be contrary to the rules of international law applicable in armed conflict, and in particular the principles and rules of humanitarian law;
>
> However, in view of the current state of international law, and of the elements of fact at its disposal, the Court cannot conclude definitively whether the threat or use of nuclear weapons would be lawful or unlawful in an extreme circumstance of self-defence, in which the very survival of a State would be at stake;
>
> In Favour: President Bedjaoui; Judges Ranjeva, Herczegh, Shi, Fleischhauer, Vereshchetin, Ferrari Bravo;
>
> Against: Vice-President Schwebel; Judges Oda, Guillaume, Shahabuddeen, Weeramantry, Koroma, Higgins.

F. Unanimously,

> There exists an obligation to pursue in good faith and bring to a conclusion negotiations leading to nuclear disarmament in all its aspects under strict and effective international control.

The two central results of the case are the general illegality of threat or use of nuclear weapons, especially in view of humanitarian law protecting civilians and combatants from indiscriminate and unnecessary effects of warfare, and the obligation to eliminate nuclear weapons through good faith negotiation. But there is much else of significance, including the Court's holdings regarding the environment, necessity and proportionality, and threat, as well as its failure to reach a definitive conclusion as to an extreme circumstance of self-defence involving the very survival of a state. The Court's conclusions must be placed in the context of its underlying analysis, for it is the opinion as a whole that describes the legal framework governing nuclear weapons. Indeed, in an unusual step, the Court made clear that its reply to the General Assembly is not restricted to the conclusions stated in the dispositif, but rather "rests on the totality of the legal grounds" set forth in the opinion, "each of which is to be read in the light of the others."[48]

As explained in the following chapters, the Court considered both treaty-based and custom-based international law. Treaty-based or "conventional" law is articulated by formal agreements among states like the United Nations Charter, the supreme treaty in the world, the Hague Conventions, an early codification of humanitarian law, and the Nuclear Non-Proliferation Treaty. It binds only those states which are parties to the relevant instruments. "Customary" law refers to universally binding law based on a general and consistent practice of states followed out of a sense of legal obligation. Treaties, especially multilateral treaties to which many states are parties, are among the official acts of states that evidence a general and consistent practice accepted as law. However, as the Court's analysis regarding humanitarian law and environmental law illustrates, a state is bound by a customary rule or principle regardless of whether it is a party to a treaty evidencing and expressing that rule or principle. Some customary rules and principles embody fundamental moral considerations, as the Court's analysis of humanitarian law reflects. Also, the Court's statute authorizes it to apply, in addition to treaties and customs, "general principles of law" widely recognized in national legal systems. While the details and mechanics of integration vary among states, all consider both conventional and customary international law to be part of their national legal systems.

♦ Chapter Seven ♦

Absence of a Specific Authorization or Prohibition of the Threat or Use of Nuclear Weapons as Such

Nothing in international law, the Court concluded in paragraph 2A of the dispositif, specifically authorizes threat or use of nuclear weapons. However, the Court attached little significance to this conclusion, noting that the legality of threat or use of any weapon is not "dependent on a specific authorization," and analyzing legality throughout the opinion in terms of whether threat or use of nuclear weapons is prohibited.[49] In paragraph 2B, the Court concluded that "[t]here is in neither customary nor conventional international law any comprehensive and universal prohibition of the threat or use of nuclear weapons as such." To reach this conclusion, the Court analyzed treaty prohibitions on the use of poisonous, chemical, and biological weapons, and the Nuclear Non-Proliferation Treaty and other treaties regulating the possession, deployment, and use of nuclear weapons. The Court also examined possible bases for a customary prohibition, the practice of non-use of nuclear weapons since the U.S. bombings of Hiroshima and Nagasaki, and the series of General Assembly resolutions condemning nuclear weapons as illegal. In general, the Court recognized a trend in international law toward severely restricting the use of nuclear weapons, but held that it has not culminated in an express categorical prohibition.

The prohibitions of use of poisonous, chemical, and biological weapons

The Geneva Gas Protocol of 1925 prohibits the use in war of "asphyxiating, poisonous or other gases and of all analogous liquids, materials or devices," and also prohibits the use of bacteriological weapons. The Hague Regulations, Article 23(a), prohibit the use of poison or poisoned weapons. Many states argued that these provisions, long understood to prohibit the use of chemical and biological weapons, also prohibit the use of nuclear weapons due to their radiation effects. The Court did not agree, stating:

> The terms have been understood, in the practice of States, in their ordinary sense as covering weapons whose prime, or even exclu-

sive, effect is to poison or asphyxiate. This practice is clear, and the parties to those instruments have not treated them as referring to nuclear weapons.[50]

However, elsewhere the Court observed that humanitarian law, "at a very early stage," prohibited the use of chemical and biological weapons "because of their indiscriminate effect on combatants and civilians or because of the unnecessary suffering caused to combatants."[51] The Court thus recognized that the ban on use of such weapons reflects humanitarian principles that apply equally to nuclear weapons.

Noting the conventions concluded in 1972 and 1993 and now in force prohibiting the possession of biological and chemical weapons, the Court recorded the obvious fact that although "[t]he pattern until now has been for weapons of mass destruction to be declared illegal by specific instruments," there is no "treaty of general prohibition [of nuclear weapons] of the same kind as for bacteriological and chemical weapons."[52]

The Nuclear Non-Proliferation Treaty and other agreements restricting possession and use

Many states sought to establish the emergence of a rule of customary international law specifically prohibiting threat or use of nuclear weapons. Key factors said to show the requisite practice and legal opinion of states were the scores of General Assembly resolutions over three decades condemning use of nuclear weapons; non-use of the weapons in war since the U.S. bombings of Hiroshima and Nagasaki; and the illegality of possession or use of nuclear weapons in most of the world by virtue of the Nuclear Non-Proliferation Treaty (NPT), regional nuclear weapon free zones in Latin America and the South Pacific, and commitments by nuclear weapon states not to use the weapons against non-possessing states. In particular, the NPT bars possession by states parties other than the five declared nuclear weapons states, commits those states to good faith negotiation of nuclear disarmament (Article VI), and has been adhered to by virtually all states, not including, however, the threshold states of India, Pakistan, and Israel.

The Court chose to divide this argument, considering first whether there is a comprehensive conventional prohibition based on treaties and other agreements, and second whether there is a comprehensive customary prohibition based on General Assembly resolutions and the practice of non-use. Unremarkably, the first inquiry yielded a negative answer – if the matter was that clear, there would have been no reason to seek an opinion. The Court also observed that existing limits on possession and deployment of nuclear weapons, including the NPT and treaties barring the weapons from the Antarctic, outer space, and the ocean seabed, may foreshadow a future general prohibition.[53]

The Court took special note of commitments made by nuclear weapon states in connection with the Treaty of Tlatelolco establishing a Latin American nuclear weapon free zone, the Treaty of Rarotonga establishing a South Pacific nuclear weapon free zone, and the NPT. In those commitments, made in protocols to the nuclear weapon free zone treaties and in declarations with respect to NPT parties, the nuclear weapon states agreed not to use nuclear weapons against non-possessing states, subject to certain exceptions. Thus in negative security assurances made in conjunction with the indefinite extension of the NPT in 1995, the nuclear weapon states except China qualified their commitment in the case of an attack against them or their allies carried out in association with a nuclear weapon state.

The Court drew two, somewhat inconsistent, implications. One was that the commitments weigh against holding threat or use to be categorically illegal, since they seem to contemplate resort to nuclear weapons in certain circumstances.[54] Another was that the commitments, and the treaties of Tlatelolco and Rarotonga, "testify to a growing awareness of the need to liberate the community of States and the international public from the dangers resulting from the existence of nuclear weapons."[55] The Court noted in this connection the recent conclusion of treaties establishing nuclear weapon free zones in Southeast Asia and Africa. Also, in the dispositif, the Court unanimously found that "a threat or use of nuclear weapons should also be compatible with ... *specific obligations under treaties and other undertakings* which expressly deal with nuclear weapons."[56] The Court thus apparently considered assurances made to NPT parties to be binding, though they are contained only in declarations, as well as assurances made in protocols (themselves treaty instruments) to treaties establishing nuclear weapon free zones.[57]

General Assembly resolutions and the practice of non-use

Regarding the practice of non-use of nuclear weapons in war since the United States' devastation of Hiroshima and Nagasaki, the Court invoked the doctrine of deterrence as the reason why the practice cannot be considered to establish *"opinio juris"* (legal consensus among states) supporting a customary prohibition:

> [Some States] recall that they have always, in concert with certain other States, reserved the right to use [nuclear] weapons in the exercise of the right to self-defence against an armed attack threatening their vital security interests. In their view, if nuclear weapons have not been used since 1945, it is not on account of an existing or nascent custom but merely because circumstances that might justify their use have fortunately not arisen.
>
> The Court does not intend to pronounce here upon the practice known as the "policy of deterrence." It notes that it is a

fact that a number of States adhered to that practice during the greater part of the Cold War and continue to adhere to it. Furthermore, the Members of the international community are profoundly divided on the matter of whether non-recourse to nuclear weapons over the past fifty years constitutes the expression of an *opinio juris*. Under these circumstances the Court does not consider itself able to find that there is such an *opinio juris*.[58]

The seminal General Assembly resolution 1653 of 1961, "Declaration on the Prohibition of the Use of Nuclear and Thermonuclear Weapons," declared use of nuclear weapons to be "contrary to the spirit, letter and aims of the United Nations and, as such, as direct violation of the Charter of the United Nations," "contrary to the rules of international law and to the laws of humanity," and "a crime against mankind and civilization." It was passed by a vote of 55 to 20, with 26 abstentions. The negative votes came from NATO and other U.S. allies. The many subsequent resolutions reaffirming resolution 1653 were passed by increasingly large majorities. Thus resolution 46/37 D of 1991 calling for a convention prohibiting the use of nuclear weapons had 122 in favor, 16 opposed, and 22 abstentions. The non-nuclear weapon states contended that the series of resolutions represent an authoritative determination that use of nuclear weapons is illegal under existing general law. They also urged that the resolutions, together with the NPT, regional nuclear weapon free zones, and other developments, evidence the emergence of a customary prohibition of such use.

The Court did not agree. Noting that several of the resolutions "have been adopted with substantial negative votes and abstentions,"[59] the Court characterized resolution 1653 as the General Assembly's disputed application of general law to the case of nuclear weapons, not the expression of a specific customary prohibition based on a legal consensus of states.[60] "Although [the General Assembly resolutions] are a clear sign of deep concern regarding the problem of nuclear weapons," the Court stated, "they still fall short of establishing the existence of an *opinio juris* on the illegality of the use of such weapons."[61] Once more, the Court referred to deterrence as an obstacle, stating that the "emergence, as *lex lata*, of a customary rule specifically prohibiting the use of nuclear weapons as such is hampered by the continuing tensions between the nascent *opinio juris* on the one hand, and the still strong adherence to the practice of deterrence on the other."[62] However, the Court recognized that the series of resolutions reaffirming resolution 1653 and calling for a convention prohibiting the use of nuclear weapons in any circumstance "reveals the desire of a very large section of the international community to take ... a significant step forward along the road to complete nuclear disarmament."[63]

♦ Chapter Eight ♦

Constraints on Threat or Use of Nuclear Weapons Based on Human Rights, the Genocide Convention, and Environmental Law

Before analyzing law specifically governing resort to war and the conduct of hostilities contained in the United Nations Charter, humanitarian law, and the law of neutrality, the Court addressed the contentions of many states that general international law relating to human rights, genocide, and the environment prohibits the use of nuclear weapons. While declining to derive a categorical prohibition from these sources, the Court held that human rights law underlies law applicable in armed conflict, and that whether a recourse to nuclear weapons violates the prohibition of genocide would depend on the circumstances of the case. Also, in an important holding, the Court stated that protection of the environment is to be taken into account in determining legality under law governing the conduct of war.[64]

Human rights

Several states contended that, in view of the extraordinary consequences of a nuclear explosion, reaching far beyond the site of hostilities in space and time, human rights law prohibits the use of nuclear weapons by one state against another because such use would violate the rights to life, health, and a livable environment of persons in the target state and in neutral states. Most centrally, Article 6(1) of the International Covenant on Civil and Political Rights, a widely ratified multilateral treaty, provides: "Every human being has the inherent right to life. This right shall be protected by law. No one shall be arbitrarily deprived of his life." The nuclear weapon states countered that human rights instruments were not intended to regulate the conduct of warfare.

The Court held that there is a right to life during war, and that humanitarian and other law applicable in armed conflict govern whether that right has been violated:

> The Court observes that the protection of the International Covenant of Civil and Political Rights does not cease in times of war,

except by operation of Article 4 of the Covenant whereby certain provisions may be derogated from in a time of national emergency. Respect for the right to life is not, however, such a provision. In principle, the right not arbitrarily to be deprived of one's life applies also in hostilities. The test of what is an arbitrary deprivation of life, however, then falls to be determined by the applicable *lex specialis*, namely, the law applicable in armed conflict which is designed to regulate the conduct of hostilities. Thus whether a particular loss of life, through the use of a certain weapon in warfare, is to be considered an arbitrary deprivation of life contrary to Article 6 of the Covenant, can only be decided by reference to the law applicable in armed conflict and not deduced from the terms of the Covenant itself.[65]

The prohibition of genocide

The Genocide Convention prohibits certain acts committed with intent to destroy, in whole or in part, a national, ethnical, racial or religious group, as such. Several states contended that intent to destroy groups by use of nuclear weapons, as the Court summarized, "could be inferred from the fact that the user of the nuclear weapon would have omitted to take account of the well-known effects of the use of nuclear weapons."[66] The Court did not expressly evaluate this view, stating regarding a "recourse to nuclear weapons" that it would only be possible to establish intent "after having taken due account of the circumstances specific to each case."[67]

Environmental law

Numerous non-nuclear weapon states had contended that the use of nuclear weapons is barred by the provisions of Protocol I to the Geneva Conventions prohibiting the infliction of widespread, long-term and severe environmental damage as a means of warfare. Several states had additionally argued for a more comprehensive customary principle of environmental security applying in time of war as well as peace and prohibiting the use of nuclear weapons because of their consequences for the environment and vital natural resources including freshwater resources, the marine environment, biodiversity, the climate system, and the ozone layer. Environmental treaties such as the Biodiversity Convention and the Climate Convention as well as declarations of international conferences were cited in support of the principle. Notably, Principle 21 of the Stockholm Declaration of 1972 and Principle 2 of the Rio Declaration of 1992 articulate an obligation of states to ensure that their activities do not damage the environment beyond their national jurisdictions. Further, Principle 24 of the Rio Declaration enjoins states to "respect international law providing protection for the environment in times of armed conflict;" and a 1992 General Assembly resolution affirms that environmental considerations are to be taken into account in implementation of law applicable in armed conflict, and declares that "destruction of the environment, not justified by military necessity, and carried out wantonly, is clearly contrary to existing international law."[68] Malaysia invoked environmental issues in describing the importance of the case to the Non-Aligned Movement, comprising 113 states from Latin America, Asia, Africa, and Europe:

> The Movement is representative of the peoples of the world to whom this issue before the Court is of the most urgent and critical interest. We are home to a huge majority of humanity with a multiplicity of problems. Our countries are custodians of natural resources and biodiversity crucial to the continued survival of people and the planet, threatened now by the destructiveness of nuclear weapons.[69]

The nuclear weapon states objected that international environmental law generally is not intended to regulate warfare. As to the Protocol I provisions prohibiting the infliction of severe environmental damage as a means of warfare, the nuclear weapon states contended that those provisions are "new" law not reflecting existing customary law. In their view, such "new" law was understood not to apply to nuclear weapons when Protocol I was negotiated.

Regarding the Protocol I environmental rules, the Court stated that they "are powerful constraints for all the States having subscribed to these provisions."[70] The Court thus indicated that they apply as treaty obligations to the use of nuclear weapons at least by states parties to the Protocol.[71] More broadly, referring, among other sources, to Protocol I, the Stockholm and Rio Declarations, and the 1992 General Assembly resolution, the Court held that environmental considerations are relevant to the determination of the legality of use of nuclear weapons under law governing the conduct of war. The Court thus linked together environmental law, humanitarian law, the law of neutrality, and the requirements of necessity and proportionality, treating international law as an integrated whole, and powerfully reinforcing the conclusion of general illegality. Indeed, despite its apparent moderation, the Court's holding regarding obligations with respect to the environment effectively bars any use of nuclear weapons. The Court reasoned as follows:

> The Court recognizes that the environment is under daily threat and that the use of nuclear weapons could constitute a catastrophe for the environment. The Court also recognizes that the environment is not an abstraction but represents the living space, the quality of life and the very health of human beings, including generations unborn. The existence of the general obligation of

States to ensure that activities within their jurisdiction and control respect the environment of other States or of areas beyond national control is now part of the corpus of international law relating to the environment.

However, the Court is of the view that the issue is not whether the treaties relating to the protection of the environment are or not applicable during an armed conflict, but rather whether the obligations stemming from these treaties were intended to be obligations of total restraint during military conflict.

The Court does not consider that the treaties in question could have intended to deprive a State of the exercise of its right of self-defence under international law because of its obligations to protect the environment. Nonetheless, *States must take environmental considerations into account when assessing what is necessary and proportionate in the pursuit of legitimate military objectives. Respect for the environment is one of the elements that go to assessing whether an action is in conformity with the principles of necessity and proportionality.*

... The Court thus finds that *while the existing international law relating to the protection and safeguarding of the environment does not specifically prohibit the use of nuclear weapons, it indicates important environmental factors that are properly to be taken into account in the context of the implementation of the principles and rules of the law applicable in armed conflict.*[72]

♦ Chapter Nine ♦

General Illegality of Threat or Use of Nuclear Weapons Under Law Applicable in Armed Conflict

In the first provision of paragraph 2E of the dispositif, the Court concluded that "the threat or use of nuclear weapons would generally be contrary to the rules of international law applicable in armed conflict, and in particular the principles and rules of humanitarian law." The importance of this conclusion, read in light of the Court's analysis, cannot be overstated: henceforth the illegality of any threat or use of nuclear weapons must be presumed. Based "in particular" on humanitarian law protecting civilians and combatants from indiscriminate and unnecessary effects of warfare, the conclusion of general illegality also is founded on another body of law specifically applicable to the conduct of hostilities, the law of neutrality protecting the rights of states not participating in the hostilities. Another basis is the Court's holding, discussed above, that environmental considerations must be taken into account in assessing legality under law applicable in armed conflict.

Humanitarian law

The principal thrust of most states' arguments for illegality, as well as the IALANA model briefs, was that the employment of nuclear weapons is incompatible with the requirements of humanitarian law applying to the use of any weapon. As Egypt stated:

> [T]he use of nuclear weapons is prohibited not because they are or they are called nuclear weapons. They fall under the prohibitions of the fundamental and mandatory rules of humanitarian law which long predate them, *by their effects*; not because they are nuclear weapons, but because they are indiscriminate weapons of mass destruction.[73]

With the exception of France, which maintained a discreet silence on the subject, emphasizing instead self-defence, the nuclear weapon states explicitly acknowledged the applicability of humanitarian law. Rather, the United States, Russia, and the United Kingdom maintained, whether a nuclear use complied with humanitarian law would depend upon the circumstances.[74]

The Court came down strongly on the side of the non-nuclear weapon states, concluding that threat or use of nuclear weapons is generally illegal based in particular upon humanitarian law. The Court explained that "[i]n view of the unique characteristics of nuclear weapons, ... the use of such weapons in fact seems scarcely reconcilable with respect for [humanitarian] requirements" forbidding the infliction of indiscriminate harm and unnecessary suffering.[75]

Humanitarian law consists of rules and principles that regulate the conduct of warfare, seeking to strike a balance between the imperatives of war and the humanitarian impulse to moderate its savagery. Also known as the law of war or the law of armed conflict, it is codified in several important multilateral treaties, including the 1907 Hague Convention, the 1949 Geneva Conventions, and the 1977 Additional Protocol I to the Geneva Conventions.[76] The Court observed regarding these and other international instruments:

> The extensive codification of humanitarian law and the extent of the accession to the resultant treaties ... have provided the international community with a corpus of treaty rules the great majority of which had already become customary and which reflected the most universally recognized humanitarian principles. These rules indicate the normal conduct and behavior expected of States.[77]

The Court first explained and identified the key principles of humanitarian law, the prohibitions of inflicting unnecessary suffering and indiscriminate damage. The Court noted their consistency with the "dictates of the public conscience" referred to in the Martens Clause and with "elementary considerations of humanity," and described them as "fundamental" and "intransgressible":

> The cardinal principles contained in the texts constituting the fabric of humanitarian law are the following. The first is aimed at the protection of the civilian population and civilian objects and establishes the distinction between combatants and non-combatants; *States must never make civilians the object of attack and must consequently never use weapons that are incapable of distinguishing between civilian and military targets. According to the second principle, it is prohibited to cause unnecessary suffering to combatants: it is accordingly prohibited*

to use weapons causing them such harm or uselessly aggravating their suffering. In application of that second principle, States do not have unlimited freedom of choice of means in the weapons they use.

The Court would likewise refer, in relation to these principles, to the Martens Clause, which was first included in the Hague Convention II with Respect to the Laws and Customs of War on Land of 1899 and which has proved to be an effective means of addressing the rapid evolution of military technology. A modern version of that clause is to be found in Article 1, paragraph 2, of Additional Protocol I of 1977, which reads as follows:

> "In cases not covered by this Protocol or by other international agreements, civilians and combatants remain under the protection and authority of the principles of international law derived from established custom, from the principles of humanity and from the dictates of public conscience."

In conformity with the aforementioned principles, humanitarian law, at a very early stage, prohibited certain types of weapons [*e.g.,* chemical and biological weapons] either because of their indiscriminate effect on combatants and civilians or because of the unnecessary suffering caused to combatants, that is to say, a harm greater than that unavoidable to achieve legitimate military objectives. If an envisaged use of weapons would not meet the requirements of humanitarian law, a threat to engage in such use would also be contrary to that law.

It is undoubtedly because a great many rules of humanitarian law applicable in armed conflict are so fundamental to the respect of the human person and "elementary considerations of humanity" as the Court put it in its Judgment of 9 April 1949 in the *Corfu Channel* case (*I.C.J. Reports 1949,* p. 22), that the Hague and Geneva Conventions have enjoyed a broad accession. Further *these fundamental rules are to be observed by all States whether or not they have ratified the conventions that contain them, because they constitute intransgressible principles of international customary law.*[78]

The Court also invoked the Nuremberg trials, stating:

> The Nuremberg International Military Tribunal had already found in 1945 that the humanitarian rules included in the Regulations annexed to the Hague Convention IV of 1907 "were rec-

ognized by all civilized nations and were regarded as being declaratory of the laws and customs of war" (International Military Tribunal, *Trial of the Major War Criminals*, 14 November 1945 – 1 October 1946, Nuremberg, 1947, Vol. 1, p. 254).[79]

This reference served in part as an implicit but salutary reminder of the principle of individual responsibility that was the basis for prosecuting Nazi war criminals. As the International Military Tribunal famously observed, "the very essence of the [Nuremberg] Charter is that individuals have international duties which transcend the national obligations of obedience imposed by the individual state."[80] Under that principle, regardless of a superior's orders or national law, all persons, military and civilian, whatever their rank or position, are obligated to terminate their commission of, or complicity with, acts connected to the use of a nuclear weapon in violation of humanitarian and other law proscribing international crimes.[81]

States had vigorously debated the applicability of the 1977 Protocol I to the Geneva Conventions, especially its provisions regarding reprisals and the environment. Protocol I comprehensively codifies humanitarian law in light of the terrible experiences of 20th century warfare, providing detailed and strict protection of civilians. Unlike the older Hague and Geneva treaties, it has not yet been ratified by several major states, but most of its key provisions are acknowledged to reflect customary law. The Court observed that while the issue of nuclear weapons was not specifically addressed in its negotiation, to the extent that Protocol I codified pre-existing humanitarian law, it is binding on all states.[82]

The Court then confirmed that humanitarian law applies to nuclear weapons just as it does to all other weapons. "[T]he intrinsically humanitarian character of the legal principles in question," the Court stated, "permeates the entire law of armed conflict and applies to all forms of warfare and to all kinds of weapons, those of the past, those of the present and those of the future."[83] The Court further noted that no state had suggested that nuclear weapons could be used "without regard to humanitarian constraints" and quoted statements of Russia, the United Kingdom, and the United States explicitly acknowledging the applicability of humanitarian law.[84] The Court also pointed to "the Martens Clause, whose continuing existence and applicability is not to be doubted, as an affirmation that the principles and rules of humanitarian law apply to nuclear weapons."[85]

At this point the Court was poised to reach the question of legality. The Court noted that, on the one hand, the nuclear weapon states had argued that whether a use of nuclear weapons complied with humanitarian law would depend upon the circumstances. The Court quoted the United Kingdom's statement that "[i]n some cases, such as the use of a low yield nuclear weapon against warships on the High Seas or troops in sparsely populated areas, it is possible to envisage a nuclear attack which caused comparatively few civilian casualties."[86] On the other hand, the Court recorded, in the view of many non-nuclear weapon states:

> [R]ecourse to nuclear weapons could never be compatible with the principles and rules of humanitarian law and is therefore prohibited. In the event of their use, nuclear weapons would in all circumstances be unable to draw any distinction between the civilian population and combatants, or between civilian objects and military objects, and their effects, largely uncontrollable, could not be restricted, either in time or in space, to lawful military targets. Such weapons would kill and destroy in a necessarily indiscriminate manner, on account of the blast, heat and radiation occasioned by the nuclear explosion and the effects induced; and the number of casualties which would ensue would be enormous. The use of nuclear weapons would therefore be prohibited in any circumstance, notwithstanding the absence of any explicit conventional prohibition. That view lay at the basis of the assertions by certain States before the Court that nuclear weapons are by their nature illegal under customary international law, by virtue of the fundamental principle of humanity.[87]

Assessing the opposing views, the Court first observed:

> [N]one of the States advocating the legality of the use of nuclear weapons under certain circumstances, including the "clean" use of smaller, low yield, tactical nuclear weapons, has indicated what, supposing such limited use were feasible, would be the precise circumstances justifying such use; nor whether such limited use would not tend to escalate into the all-out use of high yield nuclear weapons. This being so, the Court does not consider that it has a sufficient basis for a determination on the validity of this view.[88]

In thus finding that the nuclear weapon states had failed to make the case that a "limited" use of nuclear weapons could comply with humanitarian law or avoid catastrophic escalation, the Court effectively recognized a presumption that all uses of nuclear weapons are illegal. The burden is now on the nuclear weapon states to demonstrate that even a contemplated "clean" use with "low yield" weapons is permissible. Further, no "clean" use is now possible, and "low yield" weapons are an insignificant or non-existent component of present arsenals.[89]

The Court also found that it "does not have sufficient elements to enable it to conclude with certainty" that use of nuclear weapons would violate humanitarian law in every circumstance.[90] Here the Court seemed concerned with preserving its judicial integrity, declining to provide a categorical answer in the absence of established facts concerning a concrete dispute of the sort that would be at issue in a contentious case. In determining that it would provide an advisory opinion, the Court had indicated that "under the constraints placed upon it as a judicial organ," it would not "be able to give a complete answer to the question asked of it."[91] Nonetheless, in a finding that was a primary basis for the conclusion of general illegality, the Court stated:

> [T]he principles and rules of law applicable in armed conflict – at the heart of which is the overriding consideration of humanity – make the conduct of armed hostilities subject to a number of strict requirements. Thus, *methods and means of warfare, which would preclude any distinction between civilian and military targets, or which would result in unnecessary suffering to combatants, are prohibited. In view of the unique characteristics of nuclear weapons, to which the Court has referred above, the use of such weapons in fact seems scarcely reconcilable with respect for such requirements.*[92]

The law of neutrality

Article I of Hague Convention No. 5 provides that "the territory of neutral powers is inviolable." Many states argued that fallout from nuclear explosions would inevitably and significantly affect states not participating in the conflict in violation of their neutrality rights. The United States countered that the law of neutrality is understood to preclude military invasion or bombardment of neutrals, but has never been applied to collateral damage to neutral territory for lawful acts of war committed outside that territory.[93]

In a brief analysis, the Court quoted Nauru's written argument that "the principle of neutrality applies with equal force to transborder incursions of armed forces and to the transborder damage caused to a neutral State by the use of a weapon in a belligerent State."[94] However, the Court stated only that the principle of neutrality, "whatever its content," applies to nuclear weapons as it does to any other weapon.[95] The Court also noted the view that any use of nuclear weapons would inevitably affect states not involved in the conflict.[96] Accordingly, the Court strongly indicated that the inviolability of neutral states restricts or prohibits the use of nuclear weapons in other states.

♦ Chapter Ten ♦

Constraints on Threat or Use of Nuclear Weapons Based on the United Nations Charter

In paragraph 2C of the dispositif, the Court held that a threat or use of nuclear weapons that fails to comply with the requirements of the United Nations Charter is unlawful. In its underlying analysis, the Court addressed several important topics: whether the Charter categorically prohibits the threat or use of nuclear weapons; the basic requirements for lawful exercise of the right of self-defence, necessity and proportionality; reprisals; and threat and deterrence. In particular, the Court gave the requirement of proportionality a broad interpretation, further strengthening the conclusion of general illegality of threat or use. The Court also tightly circumscribed the ambit of permissible threats to threats of a *lawful* use of force. Thus because the use of nuclear weapons is generally illegal, so too is the threat of their use. While the Court declined directly to assess the legality of deterrence, its analysis of threat indirectly but unmistakably challenges that policy.

The United Nations Charter

Articles 2(4) and 51 of the United Nations Charter state the main rules governing when a state can resort to war, traditionally known as the *jus ad bellum*, as contrasted with the rules governing conduct of warfare, the *jus in bello*, most importantly, humanitarian law. Essentially they provide that a state may engage in war only in collective or individual self-defence, and then only when the Security Council has not exerted control.

Article 2(4) provides: "All Members shall refrain in their international relations from the threat or use of force against the territorial integrity or political independence of any state, or in any other manner inconsistent with the Purposes of the United Nations." The first sentence of Article 51 provides: "Nothing in the present Charter shall impair the inherent right of individual or collective self-defence if an armed attack occurs against a Member of the United Nations, until the Security Council has taken measures necessary to maintain international peace and security."

Most states accepted that Article 2(4) prohibits the aggressive use, *i.e.* use other than in self-defence, of any weapon, including a nuclear weapon, but that it does not otherwise specifically regulate nuclear weapons. A few argued that the United Nations Charter, as a whole, a priori prohibits any threat or use of nuclear weapons; others cited the provisions of the Nuremberg Charter prohibiting "planning and preparation" of crimes against peace (aggressive war) and, arguably, of war crimes and crimes against humanity. The Court did not refer to the Nuremberg Charter in this connection, and took the orthodox view of the United Nations Charter, stating that its provisions "apply to any use of force, regardless of the weapons employed. The Charter neither expressly prohibits, nor permits, the use of any specific weapon, including nuclear weapons."[97]

Necessity and proportionality

The Court was more receptive to the argument of many states that the requirements for the lawful exercise of self-defence under Article 51, necessity and proportionality, rule out the use of nuclear weapons. These requirements limit the use of force to that required to achieve a legitimate military objective and forbid the use of measures in response to an attack that are excessive in relation to the scope of the attack. As the Court noted, "self-defence would warrant only measures which are proportional to the armed attack and necessary to respond to it ..."[98] The basic requirement of proportionality, standing alone, renders illegal the first use of nuclear weapons in response to an attack with conventional forces – a strategy that has been the declared policy of the United States and NATO for decades, and that recently was adopted by Russia.

In an important holding that reinforces the illegality of preemptive first strikes against enemy nuclear forces and of nuclear reprisals, the Court further stated that proportionality requires compliance with humanitarian law:

> The proportionality principle may thus not in itself exclude the use of nuclear weapons in self-defence in all circumstances. But at the same time, *a use of force that is proportionate under the law of self-defence, must, in order to be lawful, also meet the requirements of the law applicable in armed conflict which comprise in particular the principles and rules of humanitarian law.*[99]

Also significantly, the Court accepted that the risk of escalation must be taken into account in assessing proportionality:

> [Certain States] contend that the very nature of nuclear weapons, and the high probability of an escalation of nuclear exchanges, mean that there is an extremely strong risk of devastation. The

risk factor is said to negate the possibility of the condition of proportionality being complied with. The Court does not find it necessary to embark upon the quantification of such risks; nor does it need to inquire into the question whether tactical nuclear weapons exist which are sufficiently precise to limit those risks: it suffices for the Court to note that *the very nature of all nuclear weapons and the profound risks associated therewith are further considerations to be borne in mind by States believing they can exercise a nuclear response in self-defence in accordance with the requirements of proportionality.*[100]

Also important is that, as previously noted, in analyzing environmental law the Court held that "States must take environmental considerations into account when assessing what is necessary and proportionate in the pursuit of legitimate military objectives."[101]

In sum, proportionality requires states to employ only those measures not excessive in relation to the scope of an attack, to comply with humanitarian law, and to consider the risk of escalation and the extent of harm to the environment of present and future generations. The incorporation of humanitarian law – in particular, civilian immunity against direct or indiscriminate attack – into the requirement of proportionality effectively rules out one of the most frightening and plausible scenarios for a global nuclear catastrophe, a preemptive nuclear first strike against enemy nuclear forces.

Reprisals

Noting that "[c]ertain States asserted that the use of nuclear weapons in the conduct of reprisals would be lawful," the Court stated that it does not

> have to pronounce on the question of belligerent reprisals [*i.e.,* reprisals in time of war] save to observe that in any case any right of recourse to such reprisals would, like self-defence, be governed *inter alia* by the principle of proportionality.[102]

One element of deterrence policy, retaliatory deterrence based on the threat of second use, assumes that use or threatened use of nuclear weapons in response to a prior nuclear attack is permissible. A representative of a nuclear weapon state has contended that the Court's refusal directly to address the legality of nuclear reprisals leaves this assumption unchallenged.[103] However, this view overlooks the Court's holding that the risk of escalation and environmental considerations must be taken into account in assessing proportionality. More fundamentally, it ignores the Court's holdings that humanitarian law protecting civilians must be obeyed in all circumstances and that the requirement of proportionality incorporates humanitarian law.

Here the Court's admonition to read each of the grounds for its reply to the General Assembly in light of the others must be heeded.[104]

A reprisal has classically been defined as an otherwise illegal act, taken in response to an enemy's prior illegal act, executed with the intent of causing the enemy to cease such acts. Protocol I to the Geneva Conventions includes comprehensive prohibitions on reprisals against civilians and objects indispensable to the survival of civilians (e.g., crops, water installations) as well as the environment. As with the Protocol I rules forbidding the infliction of severe environmental damage, the nuclear weapon states had argued that the use of nuclear weapons is not governed by these provisions, which they characterized as "new" law. The Court did not specifically address this contention, but its rejection is inherent in its analysis of humanitarian law. The Court described humanitarian prohibitions of attacking civilians and inflicting indiscriminate harm and unnecessary suffering as pre-dating the invention of nuclear weapons, and as applying "to all kinds of weapons, those of the past, those of the present and those of the future."[105] The Court also stated that those rules are *"fundamental"* and *"intransgressible".*[106] Its formulation of the following "cardinal" principle of humanitarian law further clarified that it applies in all circumstances: "States must *never* make civilians the object of attack and must consequently *never* use weapons that are incapable of distinguishing between civilian and military targets."[107] *It follows that nuclear reprisals are forbidden, beginning but not ending with the reprisals contemplated by the strategy of massive retaliation that target or indiscriminately kill and injure civilian populations on a vast scale.*[108]

Threat and deterrence

Regarding the threat of use of nuclear weapons, the Court made the uncontroversial observation that any threat that is aggressive in nature or otherwise violates Article 2(4) of the United Nations Charter is forbidden. Beyond that, the Court made the important holding that a threat of a use that would violate humanitarian law is also prohibited. This is evident at several points in the opinion. The Court states in its analysis of humanitarian law: "If an envisaged use of weapons would not meet the requirements of humanitarian law, a threat to engage in such use would also be contrary to that law."[109] Also, the Court found that a threat must signal a use of force that meets the requirement of proportionality.[110] This means, among other things, that the threatened use of force must comply with humanitarian law. Finally, the Court stated that "if the use of force itself in a given case is illegal – *for whatever reason* – the threat to use such force will likewise be illegal."[111]

The Court's full analysis of threat and deterrence in the context of Charter requirements was as follows:

In order to lessen or eliminate the risk of unlawful attack, States sometimes signal that they possess certain weapons to use in self-defence against any State violating their territorial integrity or political independence. Whether a signaled intention to use force if certain events occur is or is not a "threat" within Article 2, paragraph 4, of the Charter depends upon various factors. If the envisaged use of force is itself unlawful, the stated readiness to use it would be a threat prohibited under Article 2, paragraph 4. Thus it would be illegal for a State to threaten force to secure territory from another State, or to cause it to follow or not follow certain political or economic paths. *The notions of "threat" and "use" of force under Article 2, paragraph 4, of the Charter stand together in the sense that if the use of force itself in a given case is illegal – for whatever reason – the threat to use such force will likewise be illegal.* In short, if it is to be lawful, the declared readiness of a State to use force must be a use of force that is in conformity with the Charter. For the rest, no State – whether or not it defended the policy of deterrence – suggested to the Court that it would be lawful to threaten to use force if the use of force contemplated would be illegal.

Some States put forward the argument that possession of nuclear weapons is itself an unlawful threat to use force. Possession of nuclear weapons may indeed justify an inference of preparedness to use them. In order to be effective, the policy of deterrence, by which those States possessing or under the umbrella of nuclear weapons seek to discourage military aggression by demonstrating that it will serve no purpose, necessitates that the intention to use nuclear weapons be credible. *Whether this is a "threat" contrary to Article 2, paragraph 4, depends upon whether the particular use of force envisaged would be directed against the territorial integrity or political independence of a State, or against the Purposes of the United Nations or whether, in the event that it were intended as a means of defence, it would necessarily violate the principles of necessity and proportionality. In any of these circumstances the use of force, and the threat to use it, would be unlawful under the law of the Charter.*[112]

States had hotly debated deterrence in oral argument before the Court. The nuclear weapon states urged that deterrence is essential to the maintenance of international security. France stated that "the contribution that the policy of deterrence makes to the maintenance of world peace is something undeniable."[113] Its representative further told the Court, "I should like to warn against any pronouncement which, directly or indirectly, might imply judgment being passed on a defence policy based on deterrence."[114] According to the United States, "the policy of nuclear deterrence has saved many millions of lives from the scourge of war during the past 50 years."[115] The United Kingdom stated that "to call in question now the legal basis of the system of deterrence on which so many states have relied for so long for the protection of their peoples could have a profoundly destabilizing effect."[116] In stark contrast, several non-weapon states unequivocally condemned deterrence. Indonesia stated that "deterrence has several times brought the world to the brink of nuclear war and will continue do so."[117] Costa Rica stated that "it is as difficult to establish that deterrence has kept the peace – or for that matter, has not kept the peace – as it is to prove that ghosts exist, or do not exist…. Nor can there be any guarantee that nuclear war will not occur in the future."[118] Malaysia stated regarding the deterrence rationale that this is a "clear case" where "a handful of countries arrogate to themselves, the right to assess and the right to determine what is world peace and security, exclusively in the context of their own national imperatives…. Five countries cannot arrogate to themselves forever the exclusive privilege of having their finger on the nuclear trigger."[119]

Unwilling to attempt forthrightly to resolve the deep controversy among states, the Court stated that it "does not intend to pronounce here upon the practice known as the 'policy of deterrence,'"[120] and analyzed deterrence under the United Nations Charter by simply stating the applicable requirements without drawing any conclusions.[121] However, the implications are no less profound for not being stated. Rigorously applied, the holding that a threat of a use of force that violates humanitarian and other law or the requirement of proportionality is itself illegal fatally undermines the doctrine of deterrence with respect to such central and openly declared elements as threatened first use against conventional aggression by a nuclear weapon state, threatened first use in defence of "vital interests" in confrontations with non-nuclear weapon states, and threatened massive retaliation against a nuclear attack. Thus the Court's analysis mandates immediate reduction of the level of threat through the abandonment of declared policies of threatened use of nuclear weapons and adoption of measures like those recommended by the Canberra Commission and the U.S. National Academy of Sciences as steps that should be taken in the near term, including unconditional no first use commitments, withdrawal of non-strategic systems, de-alerting, and separation of warheads from delivery systems.

♦ Chapter Eleven ♦

Uncertainty as to an Extreme Circumstance of Self-Defence in Which the Very Survival of a State Is at Stake

The Court held that the threat or use of nuclear weapons is generally illegal, particularly in view of humanitarian law. The Court also held that environmental considerations must be taken into account in assessing necessity and proportionality and compliance with law applicable in armed conflict, a holding that in light of the actual effects of nuclear explosions on the environment of present and future generations powerfully supports the conclusion of general illegality. Though the relationship of threat and use seemed open to debate prior to the issuance of the opinion, the Court also unambiguously held that under the United Nations Charter threat and use are inseparable, thus making threat as well as use generally illegal.

Based on this analysis, well founded in fact and law, the Court's holding of general illegality is very strong. However, the Court also included a statement in paragraph 2E of the dispositif of its inability to reach a definitive conclusion regarding an "extreme circumstance of self-defence, in which the very survival of a State would be at stake."[122]

There was very little in states' arguments that prepared the ground for this provision. With the sole exception of France, whose rhetoric emphasized self-defence, without, however, denying the existence of humanitarian constraints, states had fully acknowledged that humanitarian and other law applies to the exercise of self-defence including with respect to use of nuclear weapons. In fact, many states agreed with the nuclear weapon states that the principal question before the Court was whether the weapons could be used in self-defence in compliance with humanitarian and other requirements.

Thus Egypt posed the question as follows, "Even when a State has the right to resort to force, in self-defence, can it use nuclear weapons?"[123] The response of the nuclear weapon states was that whether such use would comply with the law depends upon the circumstances. The response of states arguing for illegality was exemplified by Australia's statement:

> The right to self-defence is not unlimited. It is subject to fundamental principles of humanity. Self-defence is not a justification for genocide, for ordering that there shall be no enemy survivors in combat or for indiscriminate attacks on the civilian population. Nor is it a justification for the use of nuclear weapons.[124]

The United Kingdom was the only state that made arguments relating directly to the Court's extreme circumstance/survival of the state formulation, referring to a "nuclear, chemical or biological threat" and to threatened "subjection to conquest which may be of the most brutal and enslaving character" as possible justifications for nuclear threat or use in self-defence.[125] Indeed, the United Kingdom employed language that was adopted by the Court, stating: "To assume that any defensive use of nuclear weapons must be disproportionate, no matter how serious the threat to the safety and *the very survival of the State* resorting to such use, is wholly unfounded."[126]

The Court's reasoning in support of the formulation is brief. After stating that use of nuclear weapons "seems scarcely reconcilable" with humanitarian law but that it did not have "sufficient elements" to determine that use would be illegal in "any circumstance,"[127] the Court added:

> [T]he Court cannot lose sight of the fundamental right of every State to survival, and thus its right to resort to self-defence, in accordance with Article 51 of the Charter, when its survival is at stake.
>
> Nor can it ignore the practice referred to as "policy of deterrence," to which an appreciable section of the international community adhered for many years. The Court also notes the reservations which certain nuclear-weapon States have appended to the undertaking they have given, notably under the Protocols to the Treaties of Tlatelolco and Rarotonga, and also under the declarations made by them in connection with extension of the Treaty on the Non-Proliferation of Nuclear Weapons, not to resort to such weapons.
>
> Accordingly, in view of the present state of international law viewed as a whole, as examined above by the Court, and of the elements of fact at its disposal, the Court is led to observe that it cannot reach a definitive conclusion as to the legality or illegality of the use of nuclear weapons by a State in an extreme circumstance of self-defence, in which its very survival would be at stake.[128]

As President Bedjaoui observed, this is *only* a statement of uncertainty in light of the legal and factual material available to the Court. He stated: "I cannot sufficiently emphasize the fact that the Court's inability to go beyond this statement of the situation can in no manner be interpreted to mean that it is leaving the door ajar to recognition of the legality of the threat or use of nuclear weapons."[129] *Nowhere in the opinion did the Court identify any legal threat or use of nuclear weapons.* Further, uncertainty could arise only when 1) a state is acting in self-defence; 2) an extreme circumstance exists; *and* 3) the extreme circumstance threatens the *very survival* of the defending state. It is misleading to omit the third condition, as have certain nuclear weapon states in stating that the opinion does not rule out use of nuclear weapons in "exceptional" or "extreme" circumstances of self-defence.[130] Again, the Court could not reach a definitive conclusion *only* when the *very survival* of the defending state is at risk. The indivisibility of threat and use meant that the Court was considering whether a nuclear *threat* is forbidden as a means of seeking to ensure the survival of a state faced with an actual or imminent attack by nuclear weapons or similarly catastrophic means. In the only instances of *use* of nuclear weapons in time of war, the United States' atomic bombings of Hiroshima and Nagasaki, the survival of the United States was not threatened in any way. Those bombings were unquestionably illegal because they violated the prohibitions of attacking civilians and inflicting indiscriminate harm which the Court expressly held existed prior to the commencement of the nuclear age.[131]

If an extreme circumstance implicating the very survival of the defending state does arise, *the threat or use of nuclear weapons remains subject to the "fundamental" and "intransgressible" requirements of humanitarian law*. In particular, as previously noted with respect to retaliatory and preemptive uses,[132] the following rule applies: "States must *never* make civilians the object of attack and must consequently *never* use weapons that are incapable of distinguishing between civilian and military targets."[133] In addition to the categorical and unambiguous character of that holding, it bears repeating that the Court expressly directed that each legal ground for its reply is to be read in light of the others.[134] The severely restrictive consequences of this fundamental constraint for the threat or use of nuclear weapons imply that even when the survival of a state acting in self-defence is at stake, uncertainty would arise with respect only to limited threats or uses like the postulated "clean" use of "low yield" nuclear weapons which the Court found the nuclear weapon states had not demonstrated to be legal but also did not expressly find to be illegal.

The applicability of humanitarian and other law to an extreme circumstance of self-defence involving the very survival of a state is also recognized by paragraph 2C of the dispositif, which provides that "[a] threat or use of force by means of nuclear weapons ... that fails to meet all the requirements of Article 51 is unlawful." Thus *any* threat or use must meet the requirements for the lawful exercise of self-defence, necessity and proportionality, which in turn require protection of the environment and compliance with humanitarian law. Again, as the Court stated, "a use of force that is proportionate under the law of self-defence, must, in order to be lawful, also meet the requirements of the law applicable in armed conflict which comprise in particular the principles and rules of humanitarian law."[135] Paragraph 2D also provides that "[a] threat or use of nuclear weapons should also be compatible with ... international law applicable in armed conflict, particularly ... humanitarian law." In separate statements, a large majority of the judges confirmed that humanitarian and other law applies in an extreme circumstance of self-defence involving the very survival of a state.

Thus having found that the nuclear weapon states had failed to demonstrate to its satisfaction the legality of *any* use of nuclear weapons, the Court placed an impossible burden of proof on those states to ever succeed in doing so: There must exist "an extreme circumstance of self-defence, in which the very survival of a state would be at stake," *and* the threat or use of nuclear weapons in that circumstance must comply with law protecting civilians, combatants, neutral states, and the environment from indiscriminate, unnecessary, and disproportionate effects of warfare.

Paragraph 2E refers to the "very survival of *a* state."[136] However, in the body of the opinion, the Court referred to the threat or use of nuclear weapons "by a State in an extreme circumstance of self-defence, in which *its* very survival would be at stake,"[137] limiting the uncertainty only to situations when the survival of a defending state possessing nuclear weapons is threatened. In view of the clarity of that language, as well as the strength of the Court's conclusion that threat or use is generally illegal, the uncertainty should be restricted to individual self-defence by a nuclear weapon state, not collective self-defence on behalf of non-nuclear weapon states.[138]

The opinion indicated that in declaring its uncertainty about an extreme circumstance of self-defence implicating the very survival of a state the Court was balancing the general illegality of threat or use under humanitarian law against the right to self-defence and the practice of deterrence. The Court's next holding responded to this perceived contradiction, and more broadly to the risks posed of the catastrophic use of nuclear weapons, whether legal or illegal, so long as they exist.

◆ Chapter Twelve ◆

The Obligation to Bring to a Conclusion Negotiations on Nuclear Disarmament in All Its Aspects

Immediately following its holding that the use of nuclear weapons is "scarcely reconcilable" with humanitarian requirements and its statement of uncertainty with respect to an extreme circumstance of self-defence involving the very survival of a state, the Court analyzed a matter that, strictly speaking, was outside the scope of the General Assembly request: the nature of the obligation to negotiate nuclear disarmament stated by Article VI of the NPT. The Court's conclusion, set forth in paragraph 2F of the dispositif and endorsed by every judge, was that "[t]here exists an obligation to pursue in good faith and *bring to a conclusion* negotiations leading to nuclear disarmament in all its aspects under strict and effective international control."[139] The Court's reasoning in support of this conclusion was as follows:

> Given the eminently difficult issues that arise in applying the law on the use of force and above all the law applicable in armed conflict to nuclear weapons, the Court considers that it now needs to examine one further aspect of the question before it, seen in a broader context.
>
> In the long run, international law, and with it the stability of the international order which it is intended to govern, are bound to suffer from the continuing difference of views with regard to the legal status of weapons as deadly as nuclear weapons. It is consequently important to put an end to this state of affairs: the long-promised complete nuclear disarmament appears to be the most appropriate means of achieving that result.
>
> In these circumstances, the Court appreciates the full importance of the recognition by Article VI of the Treaty on the Non-Proliferation of Nuclear Weapons of an obligation to negotiate in good faith a nuclear disarmament. This provision is worded as follows:

> "Each of the Parties to the Treaty undertakes to pursue negotiations in good faith on effective measures relating to cessation of the nuclear arms race at an early date and to nuclear disarmament, and on a treaty on general and complete disarmament under strict and effective international control."
>
> *The legal import of that obligation goes beyond that of a mere obligation of conduct; the obligation involved here is an obligation to achieve a precise result – nuclear disarmament in all its aspects – by adopting a particular course of conduct, namely, the pursuit of negotiations on the matter in good faith.*
> This twofold obligation to pursue and to conclude negotiations formally concerns the 182 States parties to the Treaty on the Non-Proliferation of Nuclear Weapons, or, in other words, the vast majority of the international community.
> Virtually the whole of this community appears moreover to have been involved when resolutions of the United Nations General Assembly concerning nuclear disarmament have repeatedly been unanimously adopted. Indeed, any realistic search for general and complete disarmament, especially nuclear disarmament, necessitates the co-operation of all States.
> Even the very first General Assembly resolution, unanimously adopted on 24 January 1946 at the London session, set up a commission whose terms of reference included making specific proposals for, among other things, "the elimination from national armaments of atomic weapons and of all other major weapons adaptable to mass destruction." In a large number of subsequent resolutions, the General Assembly has reaffirmed the need for nuclear disarmament....
> ... In the view of the Court, [fulfilling the obligation expressed in Article VI] remains without any doubt an objective of vital importance to the whole of the international community today.[140]

The Court clarified the Article VI obligation in three important respects. First, the Court held that Article VI requires states to *achieve* nuclear disarmament through good faith negotiation. Talking is not enough; the talk must lead to a precisely defined result. This holding represents an application of well-established doctrine concerning the meaning of good faith negotiation in international law.[141] It also, as the Court noted, reflects the importance attached to nuclear disarmament in many General Assembly resolutions and other international instruments. Moreover, the holding is utterly consistent with the centrality of the Article VI obligation to the bargain underlying the NPT and to the long-term viability of the non-proliferation regime. Non-nuclear weapon states agreed not to acquire nuclear weapons, and the nuclear weapon states agreed in return to assist non-nuclear weapon states with development of "peaceful uses" of nuclear power and, as provided by Article VI, to negotiate the elimination of their nuclear arsenals.

Second, the Court implicitly found that the obligation applies to all states, not only those which are party to the NPT, thus binding the handful of states who are not parties, including the undeclared nuclear weapon states India, Israel, and Pakistan. While not expressly stated, this follows from the Court's reasoning, including its statements that "[v]irtually the whole of [the international] community" has been involved in the adoption of unanimous General Assembly resolutions regarding nuclear disarmament, and that fulfilling the Article VI obligation is "an objective of vital importance to the whole of the international community today."

Third, the Court delinked the obligation to achieve nuclear disarmament from the obligation, also found in Article VI, to establish a treaty on general and complete disarmament. While the Court read the two clauses of Article VI together, referring to nuclear disarmament as an aspect of general and complete disarmament, and holding that nuclear disarmament, like general and complete disarmament, must be achieved under "strict and effective international control," it focused on the nuclear dimension and made no indication whatever that nuclear disarmament is contingent upon the establishment of a treaty on general and complete disarmament. Thus the Court rejected the suggestion of certain nuclear weapon states, made in arguments before the Court and also in NPT and other international forums, that elimination of nuclear weapons may have to await comprehensive global disarmament. The obligation rather requires the nuclear weapon states to be engaged *now* in a process of good faith multilateral negotiation leading to a "precisely defined result," that is, "nuclear disarmament in all its aspects." Further, because maintenance of the level of threat inherent in present deterrence postures is inconsistent with such good faith negotiation, the obligation reinforces the general illegality of threat or use in mandating immediate reduction of the level of threat through such measures as de-alerting and separation of warheads from delivery systems. Declarations such as those made by NATO stating or implying that existing nuclear weapon policies will be maintained for the indefinite future are wholly inconsistent with the obligation, as is the further design, development, and testing of nuclear weapons.

Altogether, the Court made it abundantly clear that fulfillment of the obligation to eliminate nuclear weapons is essential to adequately addressing the dilemmas and risks posed by the nuclear age. The strength of the Court's conviction on this matter is underscored by the fact that the Court analyzed Article VI on its own initiative. That analysis, and the unanimously adopted statement in the dispositif of the obligation "to bring to a conclusion negotiations leading to nuclear disarmament in all its aspects," now stand as the authoritative interpretation of Article VI. Together with the general illegality of nuclear threat or use, the obligation to achieve the elimination of nuclear arsenals through good faith negotiations defines the legal framework for nuclear weapon policy for the United Nations, the nuclear weapon states, and indeed every state in the world.

PART THREE

THE JUDGES' SEPARATE STATEMENTS

♦ Chapter Thirteen ♦

The Judges' Individual Views on General Illegality, the Extreme Circumstance/Survival of the State Provision, and Nuclear Disarmament

All 14 judges made separate statements.[142] Each provides insight into the Court's opinion, and many are worthy of study in their own right. Taken collectively, they evidence broad support for the holding of general illegality of threat or use of nuclear weapons, widespread dissatisfaction with the extreme circumstance/survival of the state provision, and unanimity with regard to the obligation to bring to a conclusion negotiations on nuclear disarmament in all its aspects.[143]

Ten judges effectively endorsed the conclusion that "the threat or use of nuclear weapons would generally be contrary to the rules of international law applicable in armed conflict." Seven of the 14 judges voted for paragraph 2E, which contains both that holding and the statement of uncertainty as to an extreme circumstance of self-defence involving the very survival of a state: Bedjaoui, Ranjeva, Herczegh, Shi, Fleischhauer, Vereshchetin, and Ferrari Bravo. Another three judges, Weeramantry, Koroma, and Shahabuddeen, dissented because the paragraph did not hold that threat or use is categorically illegal, and therefore can certainly be counted among those supporting general illegality. Three judges who endorsed paragraph 2E, Herczegh, Ranjeva, and Ferrari Bravo, expressed views consistent with categorical illegality. Thus six judges seemed prepared to find threat or use illegal in any circumstance, and others seemed open to that possibility.[144] Also revealing of the strength of the case for illegality is that only four judges affirmatively found that threat or use could be legal, and that only in "extreme" or "extraordinary" circumstances. That step was taken, in varying degrees, by Fleischhauer, who voted for paragraph 2E, and by three judges who voted against the paragraph, Schwebel, Guillaume, and Higgins. Another judge voting against paragraph 2E, Oda, took the view that the Court should not have replied to the General Assembly request at all.

The second element of paragraph 2E, that "the Court cannot conclude definitively whether the threat or use of nuclear weapons would be lawful or unlawful in an extreme circumstance of self-defence, in which the very survival of a State would be at stake," was intensely controversial among the judges. All told, from varying angles, directly or indirectly, ten members of the Court were critical of the extreme circumstance/survival of the state formulation.[145] In contrast to the broadly supported holding of general illegality, it likely will not stand the test of time. Importantly, a large majority of the judges specifically affirmed that humanitarian and other law apply in all circumstances,[146] and only one judge, Guillaume, argued that in an extreme circumstance of self-defence implicating the survival of a state humanitarian requirements can be discounted or disregarded. Accordingly, it is clear that humanitarian law, the law of neutrality, environmental law, and the requirements of necessity and proportionality all govern threat or use in all circumstances, as was indeed provided by paragraphs 2C and 2D of the dispositif as well as the Court's categorical formulation of the humanitarian requirement of discrimination between civilians and military targets ("States must *never* make civilians the object of attack ...").

Only four judges indicated support for the extreme circumstance/survival of the state provision in separate statements, Bedjaoui, Fleischhauer, Guillaume, and Vereshchetin. Both Bedjaoui and Fleischhauer characterized humanitarian law and self-defence as competing elements, echoing the rationale supplied in the opinion.[147] Bedjaoui observed:

> Nuclear weapons can be expected – in the present state of scientific development at least – to cause indiscriminate victims among combatants and non-combatants alike, as well as unnecessary suffering among both categories. *The very nature of this blind weapon therefore has a destabilizing effect on humanitarian law which regulates discernment in the type of weapon used. Nuclear weapons, the ultimate evil, destabilize humanitarian law which is the law of the lesser evil. The existence of nuclear weapons is therefore a challenge to the very existence of humanitarian law,* not to mention their long-term effects of damage to the human environment, in respect to which the right to life can be exercised.[148]

Identifying both the right to self-defence and humanitarian requirements as fundamental in character, Bedjaoui stated:

> [S]elf-defence – if exercised in extreme circumstances in which the very survival of a State is in question – cannot engender a situation in which a State would exonerate itself from compliance with the *"intransgressible"* norms of international humanitarian law. In certain circumstances, therefore, a relentless opposition can arise, a head-on collision of fundamental principles, neither

one of which can be reduced to the other. The fact remains that the use of nuclear weapons by a State in circumstances in which its survival is at stake risks in its turn endangering the survival of all mankind, precisely because of the inextricable link between terror and escalation in the use of such weapons. It would thus be quite foolhardy unhesitatingly to set the survival of a State above all other considerations, in particular above the survival of mankind itself.[149]

Bedjaoui denied that the statement of uncertainty in any way gives states "license" to use or threaten to use nuclear weapons in an extreme circumstance of self-defence involving the very survival of the state.[150] He observed that the opinion reflects "a current trend towards the replacement of one rule of international law by another," *i.e.*, the illegality in any circumstance of threat or use of nuclear weapons, "where the first is already defunct and its successor does not yet exist."[151] He added, "States should not, in my view, see in this any authorization whatever to act as they please."[152]

Fleischhauer stated that humanitarian and other law applicable in armed conflict and the right of self-defence "are through the very existence of the nuclear weapon in sharp opposition to each other," and that "international law has so far not developed ... a norm on how these principles can be reconciled in the face of the nuclear weapon."[153] He acknowledged that:

> The nuclear weapon is, in many ways, the negation of the humanitarian considerations underlying the law applicable in armed conflict and of the principle of neutrality. The nuclear weapon cannot distinguish between civilian and military targets. It causes immeasurable suffering. The radiation released by it is unable to respect the territorial integrity of a neutral State.[154]

Nonetheless, he argued, "although recourse to nuclear weapons is scarcely reconcilable with humanitarian law," threat or use could be justified in self-defence as a "last resort against an attack with nuclear, chemical or bacteriological weapons or otherwise threatening the very existence of the victimized State."[155] Lawful exercise of the right of self-defence, he further specified, would require proportionality, and "[t]he margin that exists for considering that a particular threat or use of nuclear weapons could be lawful is therefore extremely narrow."[156]

Like Bedjaoui and Fleischhauer, Guillaume endorsed the implicit contradiction between self-defence and humanitarian law underlying the extreme circumstance/survival of the state provision, but voted against paragraph 2E because the primacy of self-defence was not recognized. Ignoring that virtually all states appearing before the Court had affirmed, and no state had denied, that humanitarian law governs the use of force in self-defence, he stated that humanitarian and other international law "cannot deprive a State of the right to resort to nuclear weapons if such action constitutes the ultimate means by which it can guarantee its survival."[157] He characterized the opinion as having concluded that in such circumstances "the law provided no guide for States," and, in a view shared by no other judge, added that, "But if the law is silent in this case, States remain free to act as they intend."[158] Acknowledging that nuclear weapons "are nevertheless 'potentially catastrophic,'" Guillaume stated that "I fully approve" of the Court's reference to the Article VI obligation.[159]

Vereshchetin defended the Court's failure to reach a definitive conclusion as to an extreme circumstance of self-defence involving the very survival of a state, stating that in an advisory opinion, as opposed to a contentious case, the ICJ should not act as a "legislator."[160] He added that while the Court could have "deduced" from humanitarian and other law "a general rule comprehensively proscribing the threat or use of nuclear weapons, without leaving room for any 'grey area,'" existing prohibitions on biological and chemical weapons of mass destruction had been established by treaty, pointing towards the most appropriate course of action for nuclear weapons.[161] Further, "the Court must be concerned about the authority and effectiveness of the 'deduced' general rule with respect to the matter on which the States are so fundamentally divided."[162] He concluded:

> [T]he construction of the solid edifice for the total prohibition of the use of nuclear weapons is not yet complete. This, however, is not because of the lack of building materials, but rather because of the unwillingness and objections of a sizable number of the builders of this edifice. If this future edifice is to withstand the test of time and the vagaries of the international climate, it is the States themselves – rather than the Court with its limited building resources – that must shoulder the burden of bringing the construction process to completion. At the same time, the Court has clearly shown that the edifice of the total prohibition on the threat or use of nuclear weapons is being constructed and a great deal has already been achieved.[163]

Apart from Bedjaoui, Fleischhauer, Guillaume, and Vereshchetin, other judges were critical of the Court's uncertainty regarding an extreme circumstance of self-defence involving the very survival of a state. In a magisterial dissent of nearly 100 pages, Weeramantry explained that he voted against paragraph 2E because the "undoubted right of the state that is attacked to use all the weaponry available to it for the purpose of repulsing the aggressor ... holds only *so long as such weapons do not violate the fundamental rules of warfare."*[164] Further, "once the domain of force is entered ... the humanitarian laws of war take over and govern all who participate, assailant and victim alike."[165] Weeramantry emphasized the supremacy of humanitarian law with regard to any threat or use, including the threat inherent in deterrence justified as a system of international security:

> The threat of use of a weapon which contravenes the humanitarian laws of war does not cease to contravene those laws of war merely because the overwhelming terror it inspires has the psychological effect of deterring opponents. This Court cannot endorse a pattern of security that rests upon terror. In the dramatic language of Winston Churchill, speaking to the House of Commons in 1955, we would then have a situation where, "Safety will be the sturdy child of terror and survival the twin brother of annihilation." A global regime which makes safety the result of terror and can speak of survival and annihilation as twin alternatives makes peace and the human future dependent upon terror. This is not a basis for world order which this Court can endorse. This Court is committed to uphold the rule of law, not the rule of force or terror, and the humanitarian principles of the laws of war are a vital part of the international rule of law which this Court is charged to administer.[166]

Weeramantry's dissent deserves to be widely circulated as a primer on the illegality of nuclear weapons. Replete with citations from the literature and jurisprudence of many cultures, Weeramantry comprehensively discussed the facts and the law rendering nuclear weapons illegal in all aspects, patiently and convincingly rebutting every argument advanced by the nuclear weapon states in support of legality. Addressing the argument that "collateral damage" caused by nuclear weapons targeted against military objectives is not prohibited, Weeramantry stated that those who use nuclear weapons "cannot in any coherent legal system avoid legal responsibility" for the consequences, "any less than a man careering in a motor vehicle at a hundred and fifty kilometres per hour through a crowded market can avoid responsibility for the resulting deaths on the ground that he did not intend to kill the particular persons who died."[167] While regretting that the Court's opinion did not go the last mile, Weeramantry began by stating that it "contains positive pronouncements of significant value" which "take the law far on the road towards total prohibition."[168] If the history of law is the history of the progression from dissent to norm, Weeramantry's opinion could be a harbinger of things to come.

Shahabuddeen rejected any suggestion that "humanitarian law provides for an exception to accommodate" an extreme circumstance involving the very survival of a state.[169] "That view," he stated, "has long been discarded; as the Court itself recalls, the [nuclear weapon states] themselves do not advocate it."[170] Citing an Islamic commentator, Ibn Khaldun, to the effect that laws "are based upon the effort to preserve civilization,"[171] Shahabuddeen emphasized the risk of nuclear escalation and denied that there is "anything in the sovereignty of a State which would entitle it to embark on a course of action which could effectively wipe out the existence of all States by ending civilization and annihilating mankind."[172] Shahabuddeen noted that the Court confronted the dilemma that to hold that states have a right to use nuclear weapons would endorse this possibility, and yet to deny the existence of such a right may seem to contradict the "principle, relied on by some States, to the effect that States have a sovereign right to do whatever is not prohibited under international law."[173] He commented:

> The dilemma recalls that which confronted the learned judges of Persia when, asked by king Cambyses whether he could marry his sister, they made prudent answer "that though they could discover no law which allowed brother to marry sister, there was undoubtedly a law which permitted the king of Persia to do what he pleased." See *Herodotus, The Histories*, tr. Aubrey de Sélincourt (Penguin Books, 1959), p. 187. So here, an affirmative answer to the General Assembly's question [whether nuclear threat or use is permissible] would mean that, while the Court could discover no law allowing a State to put the planet to death, there is undoubtedly a law which permits the State to accomplish the same result through an exercise of its sovereign powers.[174]

Koroma objected to the extreme circumstance/survival of the state provision on the ground that the right of self-defence "exists within and not outside or above the law."[175] In his view, "based on the existing law and the available evidence ... the use of nuclear weapons in any circumstance would be unlawful under international law."[176] Koroma emphasized the "weight and abundance" of evidentiary material before the Court,[177] and recounted moving testimony about the effects of nuclear weapons by the mayors of Hiroshima and Nagasaki and the Marshall Islands delegation.[178] While recording his disagreement with the extreme circumstance/survival of the state provision, Koroma also observed that the "positive findings" contained in the Court's opinion "should be regarded as a step forward in the historic process of imposing legal restraints in armed conflicts."[179]

Ranjeva stated that humanitarian principles "were intended to be applied in all cases of conflict without any particular consideration of the status of the parties to the conflict – whether they were victims or aggressors."[180] In addition to humanitarian requirements, he pointed to the "advent of an ecological and environmental order which would tend to impose itself on the nuclear order."[181] He also observed that the "law of nuclear weapons" is "inconceivable without a minimum of ethical requirements expressing the values" of the international community, including the "survival of mankind and of civilization."[182] Ranjeva's view was that "[t]here is no longer any permissible doubt about the illegality of the threat or use of nuclear weapons."[183] Regarding his vote for paragraph 2E, he explained:

> [I]f the two clauses of paragraph E had appeared as separate paragraphs, I would have voted without hesitation in favour of the first clause [general illegality] and, if the provisions of the Statute and the Rules of the Court so allowed, I would have abstained on the second clause [extreme circumstance/survival of the state]. The joinder of these two proposals caused me to vote in all conscience in favour of the whole, for the essential element of the law is safe and the prohibition of nuclear weapons is a question of the responsibility of all and everyone, the Court having made its modest contribution by questioning each subject and actor of international life on the basis of the law. I hope that no jurisdiction will ever have to rule on the basis of the second clause of paragraph E.[184]

Herczegh stated that "it is not easy to reconcile" the extreme circumstance/survival of the state formulation with the Court's holding that the exercise of self-defence is subject to the requirements of necessity and proportionality.[185] Notwithstanding this objection and his view that nuclear threat or use is "unequivocally prohibited" by humanitarian law,[186] Herczegh voted for paragraph 2E to avoid "taking a negative position on certain essential conclusions."[187]

Though neither addressed paragraph 2E directly, both Shi and Ferrari Bravo criticized the opinion's treatment of deterrence, which was one basis for the extreme circumstance/survival of the state provision. Shi stated that the practice of deterrence

> is within the realm of international politics, not that of law. It has no legal significance from the standpoint of the formation of a customary rule prohibiting the use of nuclear weapons as such. Rather, the policy of nuclear deterrence should be an object of regulation by law, not *vice versa*.[188]

He also objected to the opinion's reliance on the practice of "'an appreciable section of the international community' adhering to the policy of deterrence" because the states involved "by no means constitute[] a large proportion" of the membership of that community, which "is built on the principle of sovereign equality."[189]

Ferrari Bravo stated that "the idea of nuclear deterrence has no legal force"[190] and has served only to prevent the "implementation" of a prohibition of nuclear weapons originating in the unanimously adopted 1946 General Assembly resolution envisioning "the elimination from national armaments of atomic weapons and of all other major weapons adaptable to mass destruction."[191] In his view, "the whole of the rule-making production of the last 50 years, particularly with regard to the humanitarian law of armed conflict, is irreconcilable with the technological development" of nuclear weapons.[192]

While not taking a position on legality or illegality, Oda stated: "The equivocations of sub-paragraph E prove my point that it would have been prudent for the Court to decline from the outset to give any opinion at all in the present case."[193] Oda was the only dissenter from the decision to reply to the General Assembly request, on numerous grounds, including the role of citizens' groups in bringing the question before the Court and the question's political nature, resolvable, he maintained, only through negotiation.

Finally, Higgins and Schwebel both criticized the extreme circumstance/survival of the state provision as a failure of the Court to answer the question put to it. Higgins rejected the idea of an irreconcilable contradiction between humanitarian law and the right of self-defence, stating: "Through this formula of non-pronouncement the Court necessarily leaves open the possibility that a use of nuclear weapons contrary to humanitarian law might nonetheless be lawful. This goes beyond anything that was claimed by the nuclear weapons States ..."[194] She noted that "the Court hopes for a negotiated and verified total disarmament, including nuclear disarmament," and added, "But it cannot be the absence of this goal which means that international law has no answer to give on the use of nuclear weapons in self-defence."[195] Schwebel complained that the formulation was an "astounding conclusion" that "on the supreme issue of the threat or use of force in our age [the Court] has no opinion."[196]

Higgins and Schwebel both recognized humanitarian limits on nuclear warfare, but found it conceivable that threat or use of nuclear weapons could nonetheless be legal. They were joined in this position by Fleischhauer, as described above, and Guillaume.

Schwebel began by observing that the case "presents a titanic tension between State practice," namely, the practice of deterrence, and "legal principle," in particular, "principles of international humanitarian law which antedate that practice...."[197] He acknowledged that "it is extraordinarily difficult to reconcile the use – at any rate, some uses – of nuclear weapons with the application of those principles."[198] Schwebel therefore purported to endorse the holding of general illegality based on principles of humanitarian law, "above all, proportionality in the application of force, and discrimination between military and civilian targets,"[199] but found the principles to be quite flexible in application. He declared a "countervalue" nuclear attack on cities and industry, as distinguished from a "counterforce" attack on nuclear forces and installations, to be illegal, stating:

> It cannot be accepted that the use of nuclear weapons on a scale which would – or could – result in the deaths of many millions in indiscriminate inferno and by far-reaching fallout, have profoundly pernicious effects in space and time, and render uninhabitable much or all of the earth, could be lawful.[200]

Yet Schwebel failed also clearly to condemn a counterforce attack, though it is well known that the scale of civilian death is comparable in either a "counterforce" or "countervalue" attack as those strategies have usually been defined.[201] In a tactic typical of those seeking to divert attention from the main uses contemplated in existing strategies, he contended that "the use of a nuclear depth-charge to destroy a nuclear submarine that is about to fire nuclear missiles" would be permissible.[202] Ignoring the uncontrollable effects of radioactivity in space and time, he suggested that "the use of nuclear weapons to destroy an enemy army situated in a desert" could be legal in "certain circumstances."[203] Even if use of nuclear weapons is assumed to be prohibited, he maintained, an exception based on the law governing reprisals permits their use in response to prior use of weapons of mass destruction.[204] Here Schwebel's position is contrary to the fundamental rule protecting civilians in all circumstances from direct or indiscriminate attacks. More broadly, it is contrary to the unmistakable trend in international law toward the prohibition of reprisals targeting or harming civilians, as evidenced by Protocol I to the Geneva Conventions, and their prohibition altogether in the case of weapons of mass destruction. While the Biological Weapons Convention is not explicit on this point, few would contend that such weapons can be used in reprisal, and certainly not against or affecting civilians. As Schwebel recognized, the Chemical Weapons Convention bars reprisals by requiring that states "never under any circumstances" use such weapons.[205]

Higgins and Guillaume both implausibly assumed that the fundamental requirement recognized by the Court that states "must never use weapons that are incapable of distinguishing between civilian and military targets" does not necessarily rule out most or all uses of nuclear weapons.[206] Instead, they focused on the humanitarian law concepts of "unnecessary suffering" and "collateral damage," which they found to be somewhat elastic. Higgins stated:

> [E]ven a legitimate target may not be attacked if the collateral civilian casualties would be disproportionate to the specific military gain from the attack. One is inevitably led to the question of whether, if a target is legitimate and the use of a nuclear weapon is the only way of destroying that target, any need can ever be so necessary as to occasion massive collateral damage upon civilians.
>
> It must be that, in order to meet the legal requirement that a military target may not be attacked if collateral civilian casualties would be excessive in relation to the military advantage, the "military advantage" must indeed be one related to the very survival of a State or the avoidance of infliction (whether by nuclear or other weapons of mass destruction) of vast and severe suffering on its own population; and that no other means of eliminating this military target be available.[207]

Similarly, Guillaume asserted:

> [N]uclear weapons could not be regarded as illegal by the sole reason of the suffering which they are likely to cause. Such suffering must still be compared with the "military advantage anticipated" or with the "military objectives" pursued. With regard to nuclear weapons of mass destruction, it is clear however that the damage which they are likely to cause is such that their use could not be envisaged except in extreme cases.[208]

All 14 judges voted for the paragraph 2F statement of the obligation to bring to a conclusion negotiations on nuclear disarmament in all its aspects, and the separate statements reveal only a few mild reservations or qualifications. Schwebel doubted whether it had been established that the obligation applies to states not parties to the NPT; Guillaume and Higgins implicitly sought to preserve a possible linkage between nuclear and conventional disarmament; and several judges noted that the holding is outside the terms of the General Assembly request. On the whole, the separate statements were strongly supportive of paragraph 2F, none more eloquently than that of President Bedjaoui.

Near the beginning of his declaration, Bedjaoui wrote:

> With nuclear weapons, humanity is living on a kind of suspended sentence. For half a century now these terrifying weapons of mass destruction have formed part of the *human condition*. Nuclear weapons have entered into all calculations, all scenarios, all plans. Since Hiroshima, on the morning of 6 August

1945, fear has gradually become man's first nature. His life on earth has taken on the aspect of what the Koran calls a "long nocturnal journey," like a nightmare whose end he can not yet foresee.[209]

Addressing the Court's role, Bedjaoui observed:

> Humanity is subjecting itself to a perverse and unremitting nuclear blackmail. The question is how to put a stop to it. The Court had a duty to play its part, however small, in this rescue operation for humanity, bearing in mind the limits imposed upon it by both its Statute and by the applicable international law.
> ... It is to be hoped that the international community will give the Court credit for having carried out its mission – even if its reply may seem unsatisfactory – and will endeavor as quickly as possible to correct the imperfections of an international law which is ultimately no more than the creation of the States themselves.[210]

Invoking the fifty year history of unanimous General Assembly resolutions calling for elimination of nuclear arsenals, Bedjaoui asserted that the obligation "to negotiate in good faith and to achieve the desired result" of nuclear disarmament is now a *"general obligation, opposable erga omnes,"* that is, binding all states, including those few not parties to the NPT.[211] Noting the "very close link between this question [of nuclear disarmament] and the question of the legality or the illegality of the threat or use of nuclear weapons," he stressed "the great importance of the goal to be attained, particularly in view of the uncertainties which still persist."[212] Bedjaoui concluded:

> The solution arrived at in this Advisory Opinion frankly states the legal reality, while faithfully expressing and reflecting the hope, shared by all, peoples and States alike, that *nuclear disarmament will always remain the ultimate goal of all action in the field of nuclear weapons, that the goal is no longer utopian and that it is the duty of all to seek to attain it more actively than ever.* Human destiny depends on the will to make this commitment, for as Albert Einstein wrote, "The fate of humanity will be the one it deserves."[213]

Conclusion

In the main, the advisory opinion vindicates the efforts and hopes of the citizens' organizations and states which campaigned for years to put the question of nuclear weapons before the International Court of Justice. Despite the presence of five judges from the nuclear weapon states and two judges from NATO states, the Court ignored the objections of nuclear weapons states and answered the General Assembly's question; affirmed that like any other weapon, the nuclear weapon is subject to the law; found that nuclear threat or use is generally illegal; and affirmed the obligation to achieve nuclear disarmament in all its aspects. However, the Court also acknowledged the reality of the power and intransigence of the nuclear weapon states, declining to find that the General Assembly resolutions, opposed by those states and their allies, establish categorical illegality. On balance, the Court took an assertive role with respect to the central security issues of our time, reinforcing its importance within the system of international institutions that must function more and more effectively if the nuclear and other problems besetting the planet are to be solved. The Court's intervention in the nuclear debate was especially noteworthy in the following respects.[214]

First, the Court made a strong statement of the law governing the threat or use of nuclear weapons. The Court recognized that well established rules and principles of humanitarian law apply, most centrally that "States must *never* make civilians the object of attack and must consequently *never* use weapons that are incapable of distinguishing between civilian and military targets."[215] Moreover, in a far-reaching holding, the Court stated that impact on the environment must be taken into account in assessing legality. When combined with the Court's recognition of the "unique characteristics" of nuclear weapons, including "powerful and prolonged radiation" and destructive power that "cannot be contained in either space or time," these holdings powerfully reinforce the Court's conclusion of general illegality, and in fact further imply that *any* nuclear threat or use would be contrary to law.

Second, the Court effectively delegitimized deterrence as currently practiced, and indeed effectively condemned the entire nuclear age since it began with the United States' atomic bombings of Hiroshima and Nagasaki. The holding of general illegality, while qualified by inability to reach a definitive conclusion as to an extreme circumstance of self-defence involving the very survival of a state, clearly rules out most uses and threats. The incinerations of Hiroshima and Nagasaki, which killed over 200,000 civilians, unquestionably did not distinguish between military targets and civilians, nor was the survival of the United States at issue. Threats of first use to defend "vital interests" in conflicts with non-nuclear weapon states are prohibited. Threats of first use in response to conventional attack by a nuclear weapon state are also forbidden.[216] Threats of massive retaliation against nuclear attack are ruled out as well. All these threats and more are part of the declared postures of nuclear weapon states. Hence compliance with the law requires an immediate and drastic reduction in the level of threat and risk inherent in deterrence policies as well as expeditious implementation of the obligation to achieve nuclear disarmament. Here the opinion strongly supports implementation of near-term measures recommended by the Canberra Commission on the Elimination of Nuclear Weapons and the U.S. National Academy of Sciences, including unconditional no first use commitments; withdrawal of non-strategic weapons; taking nuclear forces off alert; and separation of warheads from delivery systems.

Third, the Court forcefully identified the elimination of nuclear weapons as the true solution to the risk of planetary catastrophe posed by the very existence of those weapons. In so doing, the Court recognized the mandatory, universal, and unqualified character of the obligation to negotiate nuclear disarmament set forth by Article VI of the Nuclear Non-Proliferation Treaty. *The Court's analysis is now the authoritative interpretation of Article VI.* It will be an important tool as non-nuclear weapon states and the global public pressure the nuclear weapon states to fulfill their obligation, as stated by the Court, "*to bring to a conclusion* negotiations on nuclear disarmament in all its aspects."[217] In a resolution supported by 115 states in December 1996, the General Assembly called for compliance with the opinion by commencement of negotiations leading towards a nuclear weapons convention.[218] IALANA, its U.S. affiliate, the Lawyers' Committee on Nuclear Policy, the International Network of Engineers and Scientists Against Proliferation, and others have demonstrated the feasibility of this approach by drafting a convention to abolish nuclear weapons modeled on the existing chemical and biological weapons conventions. It was presented to states meeting in New York in April 1997 to review implementation of the NPT as the logical and practical means of achieving nuclear disarmament in all its aspects.

Fourth, the success of the entire project to obtain an opinion from the Court signals a new level of influence of citizens' organizations over nuclear policy. The United Kingdom objected to the role of citizens' groups in the initiative, and judges Guillaume and Oda echoed that objection. These complaints served only to register the fact that civil society had found an effective means of making its presence felt within an international institution formally open only to states and U.N. agencies. For the first time the nuclear weapon states had to defend their position in an international legal forum, and politicians and diplomats the world over had to decide where they stood on the legality of nuclear threat or use. Due to the World Court Project and similar participation of civic organizations in other international processes,[219] nuclear weapons and other matters of worldwide importance are no longer solely the province of national prerogative. The global public is forcing the question of global security onto the international agenda.

The full significance of the opinion will depend on actions taken in the years ahead, as governments, militaries, and courts assess its implications, citizens' groups campaign for its observance, and negotiations proceed regarding nuclear non-proliferation and disarmament. Past ICJ cases have had an impact. In a 1971 advisory opinion, the ICJ declared the incompatibility of apartheid with the United Nations Charter, a holding that contributed to the ultimately successful campaign to dismantle that system in South Africa.[220] In the early 1970s, France discontinued atmospheric testing in Polynesia after Australia and New Zealand mounted a challenge on environmental and other grounds in the ICJ.[221] Now the nuclear weapons opinion is providing Non-Aligned Movement and other states leverage to push for nuclear disarmament, as the December 1996 General Assembly resolution illustrates. The opinion thus has already added to the momentum generated by the end of the Cold War and other developments including global outrage at resumed French testing in Polynesia, the release of the Canberra Commission report, and the 1995 award of the Nobel Peace Prize to Joseph Rotblat and Pugwash. The opinion has also created for the first time a legal framework in which citizens and present and former officials in the nuclear weapon states and their allies can demand that their governments stop treating nuclear weapons as principal instruments of national policy and start the process of their elimination. International law is now on the side of such supporters of abolition as Charles Horner, U.S. Air Force commander during the Gulf War, Alexander Lebed, Russian general and politician, and Canberra Commission members George Lee Butler, former commander of U.S. strategic nuclear forces, Robert McNamara, former U.S. secretary of defence, Michel Rocard, former French prime minister, and Lord Carver, former United Kingdom chief of defence staff.

Five decades ago, Albert Einstein warned, "The splitting of the atom has changed everything except our modes of thinking, and thus we drift toward unparalleled catastrophe." The landmark opinion of the International Court of Justice reflects that our thinking has finally begun to change, and stimulates further change. It marks and reinforces a global shift in attitudes that is making the threat, use, and possession of weapons of mass destruction the object of a planetary taboo, and points the way toward what for half a century has been practically unthinkable – the abolition of nuclear weapons.

Endnotes

[1] *Legality of the Threat or Use of Nuclear Weapons*, General List No. 95 (Advisory Opinion of 8 July 1996). Unless otherwise stated, references are to this opinion, which was requested by the General Assembly, not to the nuclear weapons advisory opinion requested by the World Health Assembly.

[2] Para. 105(2)E.

[3] Paras. 35, 36.

[4] Para. 95.

[5] Paras. 41, 42.

[6] Paras. 29, 30, 33.

[7] Para. 94.

[8] Para. 47.

[9] Para. 105(2)E.

[10] Paras. 78, 79 (emphasis added).

[11] Para. 99.

[12] Paras. 100, 103. Since the Court issued its opinion, the number of states parties has risen to 186.

[13] See Appendix B.

[14] See Appendix E for the text of the resolution.

[15] A case in Germany arising out of trespass on U.S. Army headquarters in command of nuclear weapons in Europe illustrates how the opinion can bolster the defence of protesters. While the decision acquitting the protesters has been vacated on appeal and the case returned to the trial court for further proceedings, the reasoning of the initial judge regarding the ICJ opinion is worth noting. He observed regarding the Court's uncertainty as to an extreme circumstance of self-defence in which the very survival of a state is at stake:

> Because such an extreme situation no longer exists in any case since the end of the East-West confrontation in Europe, the stationing of nuclear weapons and the maintenance of installations necessary for their

use is not (any longer) justifiable. The same is true for the related military strategy which includes still the option of the first use of nuclear weapons by U.S. Armed Forces as well as NATO.

Amtsgericht Stuttgart (District Court), Judge Wolf, B 8 Ds 1045/93, GJ 9 27928/93, B 8 (870) Cs 1039/96, B 8 Cs 1037/96, judgment dated 3 December 1996 (unofficial translation).

The opinion has also been cited in defending protesters in the United Kingdom (Reading), where an acquittal followed the prosecution's refusal to put on evidence; Belgium, where a conviction was vacated based on lack of jurisdiction; in France, where a conviction was vacated on the same ground; and in Wisconsin, Maine (the "Plowshares 8"), and Nevada in the United States. In Wisconsin, a partial acquittal was obtained; defendants were convicted in other cases.

[16] Committee on International Security and Arms Control, National Academy of Sciences, *The Future of U.S. Nuclear Weapons Policy* (Washington, D.C.: National Academy Press, 1997), p. 87 (emphasis supplied).

[17] Richard Falk comments that the Court "explicitly avoids making any legal assessment of deterrence in theory and practice. At the same time, the decision does circumscribe the legal right to threaten or use nuclear weaponry in a manner that seems inconsistent with the practice of deterrence in most of its forms, other than possibly so-called minimum deterrence. A problematic character of the decision arises from this failure to address more directly the current doctrines and practice of nuclear weapons states, which leaves in doubt the policy implications of the advice being given. Admittedly, the court was confronted by a dilemma: had it attempted to remove doubt as to the legality of current practice by making detailed commentary on strategic doctrines in various settings, it would have manifested a degree of technical incompetence that would likely have considerably damaged its reputation as a responsible judicial body." Falk, "Nuclear Weapons, International Law and the World Court: An Historic Encounter," 91 *American Journal of International Law* (No. 1, January 1997), pp. 64-75, at pp. 70-71.

[18] For the National Academy of Science recommendations, see *The Future of U.S. Nuclear Weapons Policy, op. cit.,* esp. at pp. 62-63. The Canberra Commission on the Elimination of Nuclear Weapons was convened by the Australian government and included a number of distinguished politicians, military officers, diplomats, and others from around the world. Its report was released in 1996 and is available from the government of Australia and on various web-sites, including http://www.dfat.gov.au/dfat/cc/cchome.html.

[19] See Appendix C for the text of the resolution.

[20] *Effects of Nuclear War on Health and Health Services* (Geneva: World Health Organization, 1984, 2d ed. 1987).

[21] See Appendix D for the text of the resolution.

[22] In U.N. parlance, organizations formed within civil society, for example professionals' groups providing information and advocacy on nuclear issues, are referred to as non-governmental organizations, or "NGOs." The International Association of Lawyers Against Nuclear Arms prefers not to use this term in order to stress the fact that civil society, as demonstrated, *inter alia*, by the nuclear weapons case, is coming to play an increasingly important and positive role in international affairs. Further, to define something negatively diminishes it; a state is not referred to as "non-civil society."

[23] Falk was a co-author of a 1981 paper that catalyzed a debate on the legality of nuclear weapons in the United States and the creation of the U.S.-based Lawyers' Committee on Nuclear Policy. Richard Falk, Lee Meyrowitz, and Jack Sanderson, *Nuclear Weapons and International Law* (Princeton Center of International Studies, Occasional Paper No. 10, 1981). Other members of the Tribunal were Maurice Wilkins, awarded the Nobel Prize for Medicine, and Dorothy Hodgkin, awarded the Nobel Prize for Chemistry.

[24] The full judgment of the London Nuclear Warfare Tribunal was released in 1989. Its findings included:

> 1. Any reliance on the threat or first use of nuclear weapons is a violation of international law, and constitutes a Crime against Humanity as set forth in Nuremberg Principle 6(c).
>
> ... 4. The use of nuclear weapons in a retaliatory mode, after prior armed attack and in accordance with the concept of self-defence in the United Nations Charter, is nevertheless unlawful unless such use is discriminate, proportionate, and without poisonous or unnecessarily cruel effects; since it seems impossible to satisfy such criteria, any use of nuclear weapons, whatever the pretext or justification, is an unlawful and criminal act of war entailing both governmental and individual responsibility.
>
> 5. As a consequence of (4), any form of deterrent threat to use nuclear weapons, even if limited to defensive and retaliatory situations, is a continuing violation of the laws of war; at a minimum, overcoming deterrence with all deliberate speed is an implicit legal duty for political and military leaders representing governments of nuclear weapons states.

See Keith Mothersson, *From Hiroshima to The Hague: A Guide to the World Court Project* (Geneva: International Peace Bureau, 1982), pp. 26-27; *The Bomb and the Law: London Nuclear Warfare Tribunal – Evidence, Commentary and Judgment, A Summary Report* (Stockholm: Alva and Gunnar Myrdal Foundation and Swedish Lawyers Against Nuclear Arms, 1989), p. 7-2.

[25] See Kate Dewes and Robert Green, "The World Court Project: How A Citizen Network Can Influence The United Nations," 7 *Pacifica Review* (No. 2, 1995), pp. 22-25.

[26] See Erich Geiringer, "The World Court Project: Nuclear Weapons on Trial," in *A Prescription for Global Health and Security*, Proceedings of IPPNW's Fourth Asia-Pacific Regional Conference, 4-7 August 1994, Ron McCoy, ed., 1 June 1996, pp. 22-29.

[27] See *From Hiroshima to The Hague, op. cit.*, pp. 143-149.

[28] See Peter Weiss, Burns H. Weston, Richard A. Falk, and Saul H. Mendlovitz, "Draft Memorial in Support of the Application by the World Health Organization for an Advisory Opinion by the International Court of Justice on the Legality of the Use of Nuclear Weapons Under International Law, Including the WHO Constitution," 4 *Transnational Law & Contemporary Problems* (No. 2, Fall 1994), pp. 709 – 823. Peter Weiss is co-president of IALANA, president of the U.S.-based Lawyers' Committee on Nuclear Policy (LCNP), and member of the New York bar; he also served as counsel to Malaysia and as a member of the World Court Project/IALANA legal team at the November 1995 hearings. Burns H. Weston is chair of the IALANA academic council, a member of the LCNP board of directors, and the Bessie Dutton Murray Professor of Law and Associate Dean for International and Comparative Legal Studies, The University of Iowa. Richard A. Falk is a member of the IALANA academic council, a member of the LCNP board of directors, and the Albert G. Milbank Professor of International Law and Practice, Princeton University. Saul H. Mendlovitz is UN liaison for IALANA, a member of the LCNP board of directors, and the Dag Hammarskjold Professor of Peace and World Order Studies, Rutgers (Newark) School of Law. At page 716, the article identifies numerous lawyers and others who also made contributions to the brief, many of whom participated more generally as well in the World Court Project.

[29] However, as the United States demonstrated in the case brought by Nicaragua, a permanent member of the Security Council can block that body's enforcement of an ICJ judgment. Even when this occurs, a judgment can still influence the political resolution of a dispute, as many contended was illustrated by the Nicaragua case.

[30] Mohamed Shahabuddeen, *Precedent in the World Court* (Cambridge: Grotius Publications, Cambridge University Press, 1996), p. 171.

[31] *Legality of the Use by a State of Nuclear Weapons in Armed Conflict*, General List No. 93 (Advisory Opinion of 8 July 1996).

[32] Para. 11, WHO opinion.

[33] Para. 22, WHO opinion.

[34] Dissenting Opinion of Judge Weeramantry, Conclusion, WHO opinion.

[35] Article 96, para. 1.

[36] Para. 13.

[37] Verbatim Record (trans.), 1 November 1995, p. 49.

[38] Verbatim Record, 3 November 1995, p. 59.

39 Para. 15.
40 Para. 16.
41 Para. 17.
42 Para. 18.
43 *Effects of Nuclear War on Health and Health Services, op. cit.*
44 Verbatim Record (trans.), 30 October 1995, p. 14.
45 Verbatim Record, 15 November 1995, p. 89.
46 Paras. 35, 36.
47 Para. 105(2).
48 Para. 104.
49 Para. 52. Paragraph 2A may simply have been a formal response to the question as framed by the General Assembly, whether threat or use is "in any circumstance *permitted* under international law." It could be also viewed as refusing to apply, at least in the context of nuclear weapons, a long-standing principle of international law that states are free to do what is not prohibited, and as implying that in view of the extraordinary nature of the weapons, not the absence of a *prohibition* but rather the presence of an *authorization* would be needed to establish the legality of a particular threat or use. However, paragraph 52 is contrary to such an interpretation, and while paragraph 20 briefly refers to relevant arguments of states, the opinion nowhere provides it direct support.
50 Para. 55.
51 Para. 78; see also Para. 76.
52 Paras. 57, 58.
53 Para. 62.
54 Para. 96.
55 Para. 63.
56 Para. 105(2)D.
57 See George Bunn, "The Legal Status of U.S. Negative Security Assurances to Non-Nuclear Weapon States," 4 *The Nonproliferation Review* (No. 3, Spring-Summer 1997), pp. 9-11.
58 Paras. 66, 67.
59 Para. 71.
60 Para. 72.
61 Para. 71.
62 Para. 73.
63 *Ibid.*

[64] In paragraphs 30 and 33, the Court held that environmental considerations are relevant to implementation of the U.N. Charter requirements of necessity and proportionality and of the law applicable in armed conflict, referred to in paragraph 2C, D, and E of the dispositif. That the Court's holdings regarding human rights, genocide, and the environment are not summarized directly in the dispositif is of no consequence. In addition to noting that its reply to the General Assembly "rests on the totality of legal grounds" set forth in the opinion, the Court also stated that "[s]ome of these grounds are not such as to form the object of formal conclusions in the final paragraph of the Opinion; they nevertheless retain, in the view of the Court, all their importance." Para. 104.

[65] Para. 25.

[66] Para. 26.

[67] *Ibid.* The Court did not discuss that the Genocide Convention prohibits "conspiracy" to commit genocide as well as "acts" of genocide, making it potentially applicable to plans for use of nuclear weapons.

[68] Resolution 47/37 of 25 November 1992, cited in para. 32.

[69] Verbatim Record, 7 November 1995, p. 49.

[70] Para. 31.

[71] As of 31 December 1996, Russia and China were parties to Protocol I, but other declared and threshold nuclear weapon states were not. The United States, United Kingdom, and France were active in negotiation of its text, and the former two signed the treaty at the conclusion of negotiations but have not yet ratified it.

[72] Paras. 29, 30, 33 (emphasis added).

[73] Verbatim Record, 1 November 1995, p. 39 (emphasis in original).

[74] States' arguments as to humanitarian law and other legal issues are described more fully in Appendix A.

[75] Para. 95.

[76] For more about these treaties, see Appendix A.

[77] Para. 82.

[78] Paras. 78, 79 (emphasis added). The ICJ's formulation of the humanitarian rules applicable at the outset of the nuclear age rather closely parallels that offered by Antonio Cassese in his *Violence and Law in the Nuclear Age* (Princeton: Princeton University Press, 1988), esp. at pp. 14-17. Cassese also discusses an aspect of the principle forbidding the infliction of indiscriminate harm not addressed by the Court, that requiring proportionality between "collateral damage" to civilians and the military advantage gained by the attack on a legitimate military objective. See also Dissenting Opinion of Judge Higgins, para. 20. The Court may have determined that in the case of nuclear weapons, the prohibition of use of weapons incapable of distinguishing between civilians and military tar-

gets is the most relevant aspect of the requirement of discrimination. This interpretation is consistent with the holding of general illegality.

[79] Para. 80.

[80] *United States et al. v. Goering et al. (Judgment of the International Military Tribunal)*, 6 Federal Rules of Decision (U.S.) 69, 110 (1946). On 11 December 1946, based on a proposal submitted by the United States, the General Assembly unanimously adopted resolution 95 affirming the principles of international law recognized by the Nuremberg Charter and Judgment and directing the International Law Commission (ILC) to codify those principles. The fourth principle formulated by the ILC pursuant to this directive provides: "The fact that a person acted pursuant to order of his government or of a superior does not relieve him from responsibility under international law, provided a moral choice was in fact possible for him." *Report of the International Law Commission, 2nd session*, 5 U.N. GAOR Supp. (No. 12) at 14, U.N. Doc. A/1316 (1950), reprinted in [1950] 2 *Yearbook of the International Law Commission* at 377, U.N. Doc. A/CN.4/SERA/1950/Add.1.

[81] This is only a statement of the minimal consequences of the principle of individual responsibility in the context of nuclear weapons. In light of present circumstances, the principle may require much more, for example, termination of participation or complicity in the formulation of plans or maintenance of capability for the possible use of nuclear weapons, or affirmative acts to prevent such planning, maintenance, or use.

[82] Para. 84.

[83] Para. 86.

[84] *Ibid.*

[85] Para. 87.

[86] Para. 91.

[87] Para. 92.

[88] Para. 94.

[89] According to the Natural Resources Defence Council (NRDC), in its 1997 operational forces totaling about 8750 warheads the United States has 650 warheads with a selectable yield capability involving four options, the lowest at 300 tons (.3 kilotons), the next at 1.5 kilotons (5 kilotons in one model), the next at 10 kilotons (60 kilotons in one model), and the highest at 45, 80, or 170 kilotons depending on the model. Another 400 had yield options from sub-kiloton to 350 kilotons. Another 1150 had yields of five and 150 kilotons. Most of the rest of the arsenal had yields in the low hundreds of kilotons, with some in the megaton range (more than 1000 kilotons). See "NRDC Nuclear Notebook, Table of U.S. Nuclear Weapons Stockpile, Operational Forces (July/August 1997)," *Bulletin of the Atomic Scientists* (July/August 1997), p. 63. The bombs the U.S. dropped on Hiroshima and Nagasaki had yields in the range of 12 to 20 kilo-

tons. A 300-ton warhead is an order of magnitude more powerful than the most powerful conventional explosives, and of course also releases radiation. While a 300-ton warhead may nonetheless be considered a "low yield" nuclear weapon on an absolute scale of destructive power as well as on a scale relative to nuclear weapons with yields in the hundreds of kilotons, it is hard to categorize a five-kiloton warhead as such. NRDC states that the United Kingdom also has the ability to select partial yields from one or less kiloton to several kilotons on warheads with full yields of 100 kilotons deployed on submarine-launched ballistic missiles. NRDC Nuclear Program, Nuclear Data, Table of British Nuclear Forces, end 1996, http://www.nrdc.org/nrdcpro/nudb/datab12.html. At the same website, NRDC reports that China deploys 120 warheads with yields in the "low kilotons" in artillery and other short-range delivery systems. There is no other information relevant to "low yield" nuclear weapons reported in NRDC tables for Russian, Chinese, and French nuclear forces, which all deploy warheads with yields in the hundreds of kilotons (China also has warheads with yields in the megaton range). See also "NRDC Nuclear Notebook, Estimated Russian Stockpile, End of 1996," *Bulletin of the Atomic Scientists* (May/June 1997), pp. 62-64.

[90] Para. 95.

[91] Para. 19.

[92] Para. 95 (emphasis added).

[93] Written Statement of the United States re General Assembly question, pp. 31-32.

[94] Para. 88.

[95] Para. 89.

[96] Para. 93.

[97] Para. 39.

[98] Para. 41.

[99] Para. 42 (emphasis added).

[100] Para. 43 (emphasis added).

[101] Para. 30.

[102] Para. 46.

[103] See Michael J. Matheson, "The Opinions of the International Court of Justice on the Threat or Use of Nuclear Weapons," 91 *American Journal of International Law* (No. 3, July 1997), pp. 417-435, at p. 432. Matheson is Principal Deputy Legal Adviser, U.S. Department of State, and was one of the U.S. advocates appearing before the ICJ at the November 1995 hearings.

[104] Para. 104.

[105] Para. 86.

[106] Para. 79 (emphasis added).

[107] Para. 78 (emphasis added).

[108] The U.S. National Academy of Sciences study states that plans for possible second use of nuclear weapons must be severely constrained for both prudential and moral reasons. It recommends that the United States eliminate plans for "massive retaliation" that "require prompt attacks on counterforce [nuclear weapon facility] targets or imperil major fractions of the [enemy] nation's population" and adopt plans that would "minimize civilian casualties" and use "the smallest number possible" of nuclear weapons. *The Future of U.S. Nuclear Weapons Policy, op. cit.*, p. 64. Its recommendations, if adopted, would represent some movement in the direction of compliance with the requirements of humanitarian law applying to the threat or execution of nuclear reprisals or other second use.

[109] Para. 78.

[110] Para. 48.

[111] Para. 47 (emphasis added).

[112] Paras. 47, 48 (emphasis added).

[113] Verbatim Record (trans.), 1 November 1995, p. 36.

[114] *Ibid.*

[115] Verbatim Record, 15 November 1995, pp. 86-87.

[116] *Ibid.*, p. 23.

[117] Verbatim Record, 3 November 1995, pp. 22-23.

[118] Verbatim Record, 14 November 1995, p. 27.

[119] Verbatim Record, 7 November 1995, pp. 53-54, 56.

[120] Para. 67.

[121] Para. 48.

[122] Para. 105(2)E.

[123] Verbatim Record, 1 November 1995, p. 35.

[124] Verbatim Record, 30 October 1995, p. 62.

[125] Verbatim Record, 15 November 1995, pp. 39, 48-49.

[126] *Ibid.*, p. 39 (emphasis added).

[127] Para. 95.

[128] Paras. 96, 97.

[129] Declaration of President Bedjaoui, para. 11.

[130] See statements of France and the United Kingdom quoted in Appendix B.

[131] See paras. 78, 86.

[132] The question of the legality of nuclear reprisals could arise when an enemy state has used nuclear or other weapons of mass destruction. Similarly, the question of the legality of preemptive uses could arise when it is believed that an enemy state is about to use such weapons. In some (not all) cases these questions could concern a threat to the very survival of the defending state. The separate statements of Fleischhauer and Higgins, like the United Kingdom's argument, implicitly raise these issues in characterizing an extreme circumstance as involving actual or imminent harm on the scale of that caused by nuclear or other weapons of mass destruction. Higgins referred to "defence against untold suffering or the obliteration of a State or peoples" and "the avoidance of infliction (whether by nuclear or other weapons of mass destruction) of vast and severe suffering." Dissenting Opinion of Judge Higgins, paras. 18, 21. Fleischhauer referred to "a last resort against an attack with nuclear, chemical or bacteriological weapons or otherwise threatening the very existence of the victimized State." Separate Opinion of Judge Fleischhauer, para. 5.

[133] Para. 78 (emphasis added).

[134] Para. 104.

[135] Para. 42. Paragraph 30 provides that "[r]espect for the environment is one of the elements that go to assessing whether an action is in conformity with the principles of necessity and proportionality."

[136] Para. 105(2)E (emphasis added). Fleischhauer, who voted for paragraph 2E, stated that the uncertainty applies in extreme situations of individual *or* collective self-defence, without further analysis. Separate Opinion of Judge Fleischhauer, para. 5. The separate statements of other judges do not cast much light on this issue.

[137] Para. 97 (emphasis added).

[138] The United Kingdom told the Court: "A decision to use nuclear weapons would only be taken in extreme cases and on the basis of the ultimate duty of a State to defend its people and their homeland." Verbatim Record, 15 November 1995, p. 39.

[139] Para. 105(2)F (emphasis added).

[140] Paras. 98, 99, 100, 101, 103 (emphasis added).

[141] *Gulf of Maine*, 1984 ICJ Rep. 246, 292; *North Sea Continental Shelf*, 1969 ICJ Rep. 4, 47.

[142] Judges' separate statements were variously denominated declarations (five of the seven judges who voted for all formal conclusions, Bedjaoui, Herczegh, Shi, Vereshchetin, Ferrari Bravo), separate or individual opinions (two of the judges who voted for all formal conclusions, Ranjeva and Fleischhauer, and Guillaume), and dissenting opinions (Schwebel, Oda, Shahabuddeen, Weeramantry, Koroma, and Higgins).

[143] Parts of this chapter draw on Peter Weiss, "Notes on a Misunderstood Decision: the World Court's Near Perfect Advisory Opinion in the Nuclear Weapons Case," *Medicine & Global Survival* (23 July 1997), on-line journal at http://www.healthnet.org/MGS, also available from the Lawyers' Committee on Nuclear Policy or IALANA.

[144] It perhaps is the case that President Bedjaoui was concerned to avoid an outcome which would have pitted judges from non-nuclear weapon states against judges from nuclear weapon states and their allies. As it was, judges voting for paragraph 2E include judges from Russia, China, Germany, and Italy. Bedjaoui noted in his separate statement that the vote distribution is "in no way consistent with any geographical split;" he added that "this is a mark of the independence of the Members of the Court which I am happy to emphasize." Declaration of President Bedjaoui, para. 18.

[145] Schwebel, Oda, Shahabuddeen, Weeramantry, Ranjeva, Herczegh, Shi, Koroma, Ferrari Bravo, and Higgins.

[146] Schwebel, Shahabuddeen, Weeramantry, Ranjeva, Herczegh, Fleischhauer, Koroma, Bedjaoui, and Higgins. This position also follows directly from Ferrari Bravo's analysis, and is not inconsistent with that of Shi and Vereshchetin.

[147] Para. 96.

[148] Declaration of President Bedjaoui, para. 20 (emphasis in original).

[149] *Ibid.*, para. 22.

[150] *Ibid.*, para. 14.

[151] *Ibid.*, para. 16.

[152] *Ibid.*

[153] Separate Opinion of Judge Fleischhauer, para. 5.

[154] *Ibid.*, para. 2.

[155] *Ibid.*, para. 5.

[156] *Ibid.*, para. 6.

[157] Individual Opinion of Judge Guillaume, para. 8.

[158] *Ibid.*, para. 9.

[159] *Ibid.*, para. 13.

[160] Declaration of Judge Vereshchetin, pp. 48-49.

[161] *Ibid.*, p. 49.

[162] *Ibid.*

[163] *Ibid.*, p. 50.

[164] Dissenting Opinion of Judge Weeramantry, p. 232 (emphasis in original).

[165] *Ibid.*, p. 236.

[166] *Ibid.*, pp. 259-260.

[167] *Ibid.*, p. 215.

[168] *Ibid.*, p. 170.

[169] Dissenting Opinion of Judge Shahabuddeen, p. 164.

[170] *Ibid.*

[171] *Ibid.*, p. 133.

[172] *Ibid.*, p. 141.

[173] *Ibid.*, p. 140.

[174] *Ibid.*, n.18.

[175] Dissenting Opinion of Judge Koroma, p. 267.

[176] *Ibid.*, p. 264.

[177] *Ibid.*

[178] *Ibid.*, pp. 271-274. See Appendix A, "Effects of Nuclear Weapons," for portions of this testimony.

[179] *Ibid.*, p. 280.

[180] Individual Opinion of Judge Ranjeva, p. 67.

[181] *Ibid.*, p. 62.

[182] *Ibid.*, pp. 62-63.

[183] *Ibid.*, p. 62.

[184] *Ibid.*, p. 69.

[185] Declaration of Judge Herczegh, pp. 44-45.

[186] *Ibid.*, p. 44.

[187] *Ibid.*, p. 45.

[188] Declaration of Judge Shi, p. 46.

[189] *Ibid.*, pp. 46-47.

[190] Declaration of Judge Ferrari Bravo, p. 52.

[191] *Ibid.*, pp. 51-52, 54. The reference is to resolution 1 (I) of 24 January 1946.

[192] *Ibid.*, p. 53.

[193] Dissenting Opinion of Judge Oda, p. 128.

[194] Dissenting Opinion of Judge Higgins, para. 29.

[195] *Ibid.*, para. 31.

[196] Dissenting Opinion of Vice-President Schwebel, p. 83.

[197] *Ibid.*, p. 75.

[198] *Ibid.*

[199] *Ibid.*, pp. 82-83.

[200] *Ibid.*, p. 82.

[201] See Frank N. Von Hippel, Barbara G. Levi, Theodore A. Postol, and William H. Daugherty, "Civilian Casualties from Counterforce Attacks," 259 *Scientific American* (September 1988), p. 36 *et seq.* See also declaration of Joseph Rotblat, presented to the Court by the Solomon Islands, quoted in "Effects of Nuclear Weapons," Appendix A.

[202] Dissenting Opinion of Vice-President Schwebel, p. 82.

[203] *Ibid.*

[204] *Ibid.*, p. 88.

[205] *Ibid.*

[206] Dissenting Opinion of Judge Higgins, para. 24; Individual Opinion of Judge Guillaume, para. 5.

[207] Dissenting Opinion of Judge Higgins, paras. 20-21. At the end of her opinion, Higgins expressed some misgivings, stating (para. 41):

> One cannot be unaffected by the knowledge of the unbearable suffering and vast destruction that nuclear weapons can cause. And one can well understand that it is expected of those who care about such suffering and devastation that they should declare its cause illegal. It may well be asked of a judge whether, in engaging in legal analysis of such concepts as "unnecessary suffering," "collateral damage" and "entitlement to self-defence," one has not lost sight of the real human circumstances involved. The judicial lodestar ... must be those values that international law seeks to promote and protect. In the present case, it is the physical survival of peoples that we must constantly have in view.

But she then referred to the risk of proliferation of nuclear weapons to additional states, and concluded only that "[i]t is not clear to me that either a pronouncement of illegality in all circumstances [or] paragraph 2E best serve to protect mankind against that unimaginable suffering that we all fear."

[208] Individual Opinion of Judge Guillaume, para. 5.

[209] Declaration of President Bedjaoui, para. 2.

[210] *Ibid.*, paras. 6, 8.

[211] *Ibid.*, para. 23.

[212] *Ibid.*

[213] *Ibid.*, para. 24 (emphasis in original). A translation from the French different than the U.N. version is provided for the last sentence.

[214] This conclusion draws on Peter Weiss, "One Way to ban the Bomb: outlaw it," *The Riverdale Press* (15 August 1996), p. 5.

[215] Para. 78 (emphasis added).

[216] Uncertainty could arise only with respect to a non-nuclear attack (whether by a state possessing nuclear weapons or not) that posed a threat to the very survival of the defending state.

[217] Para. 105(2)E (emphasis added).

[218] For the text of this resolution, see Appendix E.

[219] Notably the 1988 UN Special Session on Disarmament, the 1992 Earth Summit in Rio de Janeiro, and the 1996 Women's Conference in Beijing.

[220] *Advisory Opinion on the Continued Presence of South Africa in Namibia (South West Africa)* 1971 ICJ Rep. 16. The opinion concerned the legality of policies of racial discrimination in Namibia, a territory under the protection of the United Nations. Nonetheless, it was plainly applicable to the same policies in South Africa.

[221] *Nuclear Tests (Australia v. France)* 1974 ICJ Rep. 253. After France declared its intent to stop atmospheric testing, the Court dismissed the case as moot. In so doing, the Court found that France's declaration represented the assumption of a binding obligation.

APPENDIX A
States' Arguments to the Court

Introduction

More than two-thirds of the states participating in written and oral proceedings before the Court argued for the illegality of the threat or use of nuclear weapons. The basic argument of Non-Aligned Movement and other non-nuclear weapon states was that nuclear weapons are inherently indiscriminate, uncontrollable, and inhumane weapons of mass destruction, whose use is therefore prohibited by the rules and principles of humanitarian and other law applicable in armed conflict that protect non-combatants, the environment, neutral states, and succeeding generations from the effects of warfare. This law applies, they stressed, in any circumstance, including self-defence. That the law applies equally to the defender and the aggressor state was acknowledged by both sides to the debate.

The only states strongly arguing for legality were the declared nuclear weapon states of France, the United States, Russia, and the United Kingdom. Their argument was that the law applicable in armed conflict does not necessarily operate to prohibit use of the weapons in all circumstances. Whether a use is legal, they asserted, depends on the facts of each case and cannot be prejudged. Certain members of the Western nuclear-armed alliance, NATO, supported the legality argument (the Netherlands) or largely (Germany, Italy) or entirely (Finland) contended that the Court should not answer the question. Ireland emphasized its support for a political process of abolishing of nuclear weapons, but also stated that an advisory opinion from the Court concerning the legality of threat or use would not be incompatible with that process and that it awaited the Court's opinion "with interest."[1] Norway similarly stated that its "main concern" is building "lasting political commitments which will ensure that nuclear weapons will never be used" through a disarmament process and that the Court should "place great emphasis on these considerations."[2]

In the oral presentation of its Attorney General, Paul East, Aotearoa/New Zealand provided an excellent summary of the elements of law separately and cumulatively relied upon by the non-weapon states to demonstrate the illegality of use of nuclear weapons:

1. *[T]he right of the parties to an armed conflict to choose methods or means of warfare is not unlimited.* That is to say the world community rejected any doctrine of unlimited warfare or of total war. Rather, both in principle and in treaty obligations since the St. Petersburg Declaration in 1868, the world community has accepted that limit. It is a limit, of course, which flatly rejects in this area any general proposition that under international law States are free to act unless they are specifically prohibited.

2. *The second principle requires parties to a conflict to distinguish at all times between the civilian population and combatants and between civilian objects and military objectives in order to spare the civilian population and property.* Neither the civilian population as such nor civilian persons are to be the object of attack. Attacks must be directly solely against military objectives. There can of course be collateral civilian damage consequential to an attack on a legitimate military target. That realisation of the harsh facts of war is however tempered by the requirement that the loss of civilian life, injury to civilians, damage to civilian objects or any combination of those losses must not be excessive in relation to the concrete and military advantage anticipated. One member of this Court, citing an earlier President of the Court, has referred to an Indian classic, *The Ramayana*. That text tells us that the use of a weapon of war which would destroy the entire race of the enemy was forbidden by the virtuous Prince Rama. The reason given is that the weapon would destroy even those who did not bear arms; such destruction en masse was forbidden by the ancient laws of war even though Rama's adversary was fighting an unjust war…

3. *A third basic principle is that parties to a conflict must not use weapons and methods and means of warfare of a nature to cause superfluous injury or unnecessary suffering.* Again there is a recognition in this proposition that armed conflict does cause suffering. There is, however, a limit on weapons by reference to superfluity and lack of necessity.

4. A fourth principle is unlike the preceding three in that it cannot be traced back to the last century or even earlier. It has been recognized more recently as the destructive effect of weapons has massively increased. *Under this principle parties to a conflict must not use methods or means of warfare which are*

intended or may be expected to cause widespread, long term and severe damage to the natural environment. Closely related to this principle is the concern for intergenerational damage, a matter touched on by Judge Weeramantry in his dissenting opinion given in this Court two months ago when New Zealand sought to resume the case which it had brought in 1973 relating to French Nuclear Testing. That idea of a continuing obligation owed to future generations is increasingly recognized in environmental law. Indeed, it is noteworthy that over 200 years ago an American President, James Madison, espoused a not dissimilar principle when writing in the National Gazette on 2 February 1792: "Each generation should bear the burden of its own wars, instead of carrying them on at the expense of other generations."

5. *A fifth relevant principle ... is that methods and means of warfare must not violate the neutrality of States which are not participating in the conflict.* Belligerents have no right to carry on hostilities within the territory of such a State. Neutral States have the right to freedom from harm and injury arising from an armed conflict with which they are not involved.

6. *Finally is the set of rules prohibiting the use of asphyxiating, poisonous or other gases and all analogous materials.* This principle is generally acknowledged as forming part of customary international law and is codified in part in the 1925 Geneva Protocol on the use in war of gases and bacteriological weapons. Given the radiation effects of nuclear weapons many contend that this body of law also applies to nuclear weapons.[3]

The underlying rationale of law applicable in armed conflict, and its incompatibility with use of nuclear weapons, was eloquently stated by the Iranian Deputy Minister of Foreign Affairs, Mohammed Javad Zarif:

> I wish to recall Aristotle's unsurpassed definition of war: "The aim of all war is peace." In this definition he underlines, on the one hand, that war is an interruption, a temporary replacement of normalcy, or the explosion of a gradually developed disequilibrium, that must result in a new normalcy. On the other hand, Aristotle's dictum also describes the overall philosophy of the 20th century's law of war, and suggests that within a relatively short historical perspective, every war will come to an end. Hence, in the law of United Nations and in the logic of its Charter which provides a general prohibition of resort to force except in self-defence, even such legitimate use of force must be conducted in accordance with laws of war, and with the post-war situation in mind. It must not lead to disorganization so great as

to ruin even the defeated. Article 40 of Additional Protocol I [to the Geneva Conventions] prohibits exactly what the use of nuclear weapons will cause. It prohibits "to order that there shall be no survivors, to threaten an adversary therewith or to conduct hostilities on this basis." Given the uncontrollable nature of the effects of nuclear weapons, it is quite clear that their use is not aimed at achieving peace but to destroy everything, which certainly contravenes the general principles of international humanitarian law.[4]

In addition to law applicable in armed conflict, several non-weapon states contended that human rights law bars the use of nuclear weapons. A few states also invoked the Genocide Convention. Some states additionally argued that a customary international law norm has developed that specifically prohibits threat or use of nuclear weapons, based upon General Assembly resolutions, the Nuclear Non-Proliferation Treaty, regional nuclear weapon free zones, and other agreements and commitments. Others argued that the United Nations Charter generally, or its requirements of necessity and proportionality in the exercise of self-defence, rule out use of nuclear weapons. The legality of threat, as well as use, under the Charter and other law, was the subject of intense debate, because it raised the issue of the legitimacy of deterrence. States also addressed factual issues concerning the effects of nuclear weapons. The WHO studies were cited, and Japan and the Marshall Islands made dramatic and moving presentations.

States' arguments are described below under the following headings: 1) the effects of nuclear weapons; 2) humanitarian law; 3) environmental law; 4) reprisals; 5) the law of neutrality; 6) human rights; 7) the prohibition of poisonous and analogous weapons; 8) the prohibition of genocide; 9) General Assembly resolutions and the Nuclear Non-Proliferation Treaty; 10) the United Nations Charter; and 11) threat and deterrence.

The Effects of Nuclear Weapons

To make the factual case for illegality, non-nuclear weapon states referred the Court to a number of authoritative sources, notably the 1984 and 1987 World Health Organization studies of the effects of nuclear war on health and health services.[5] The Solomon Islands introduced a declaration by Joseph Rotblat, who served as rapporteur for both WHO studies. Rotblat was a member of the British team on the Manhattan Project and the only physicist to leave the Project for moral reasons, later specialized in radiation physics and biology, and is the president of Pugwash and the 1995 Nobel Peace Prize Winner. Rotblat's statement read in part:

> Of the three main injurious agents of nuclear weapons – blast, heat and ionizing radiations – one aspect of the last agent, fall-out, is the least amenable to quantitative assessment, owing to its dependence on a number of unpredictable factors. Yet, in any nuclear war, local and/or global fall-out are likely to produce a heavy casualty toll.
>
> In a counterforce attack, with the underground ICBM silos as targets, the great accuracy of modern missiles might make it possible to avoid direct hits on large centres of population, but millions of civilians are likely to be killed or suffer long-term effects of radiation from exposure to fall-out.... In an all-out war, into which any nuclear conflict is very likely to escalate, the largest immediate casualty toll would be from the effects of blast, heat and initial radiation in the cities hit by nuclear weapons. But in this case too fall-out would add immensely to the numbers of dead and injured, as well as greatly diminishing the extent of post-war recovery. Civil defence measures such as deep shelters, which may provide some protection against blast, would be [much] less effective against local fall-out, owing to problems arising from the necessary long stay in such shelters. Huge areas of land, remote from the target zones, would remain uninhabitable for long periods, probably years if nuclear reactors were targets of attack, and most of the livestock and crops would be lost.
>
> The effects of local fall-out would be felt just as badly in some non-combatant countries, but global fall-out would result

in long-term damage to *all* countries, including the Antarctic; it would be expressed in an increased incidence of cancers, and it is to be expected that there would be an increase in genetic defects in future generations. The property of fall-out to extend the injurious action both in space and in time, is a novel and unique characteristic of nuclear warfare. Not only the inhabitants of the combatant countries, but virtually the whole population of the world, and their descendants, would be victims of a nuclear war – therein lies the radical change which nuclear weapons introduce into the whole concept of warfare.

I have read the written pleadings prepared by the United Kingdom and the United States. Their view of the legality of the use of nuclear weapons is premised on three assumptions: a) that they would not necessarily cause unnecessary suffering; b) that they would not necessarily have indiscriminate effects on civilians; c) that they would not necessarily have effects on territories of third states. It is my professional opinion – set out above and in the WHO reports referred to – that on any reasonable set of assumptions their argument is unsustainable on all three points. Even in the hypothetical case that at some time in the future nuclear weapons are developed that have a negligible effect on the civilian population, any use of such a weapon is likely to start a nuclear conflict in which other nuclear weapons are used that have all the effects described above.[6]

Iran's Javad Zarif quoted the WHO 1987 report, describing it as an "excellent illustration of the effects of the use of nuclear weapons on health and the environment":

Less quantifiable effects of nuclear war include atmospheric changes detrimental to agriculture and the economy, not only in the countries where the war takes place, but also in others not engaged in hostilities. Moreover, since the world has never experienced a large-scale nuclear war, other unpredictable direct and indirect effects cannot be excluded. Any assessment of the effects of a nuclear war must therefore be attended by a high degree of uncertainty. However, on the basis of the information derived from the explosions at Hiroshima and Nagasaki, the tests of nuclear weapons and accidents at nuclear power plants, research in radiation physics and biology, and earthquakes, fires, floods, volcanic eruptions, and other natural disasters, it is possible to predict with reasonable accuracy the main effects on people and their environment. Those effects would not be limited to the people of the area where the bombs fell; some of them would be felt by people throughout most of the world.[7]

Other evidence came from states, Japan and the Marshall Islands, that have suffered the effects of nuclear explosions. Japan took an ambivalent stance reflecting the tension in that country between reliance on the United States "nuclear umbrella" and a powerful abolition movement. While saying that "the use of nuclear weapons is clearly contrary to the spirit of humanity that gives international law its philosophical foundation," Takekazu Kawamura, Director General for Arms Control and Scientific Affairs, stopped short of arguing for illegality.[8] He then presented the mayors of Hiroshima and Nagasaki to introduce evidence of their cities' horrific experiences, but noted that their statements would be made "independently of the position of the Japanese government."[9]

Takashi Hiraoka, Mayor of Hiroshima, told the Court:

> The atomic bombs dropped on Hiroshima and Nagasaki shattered all war precedent. The mind-numbing damage these nuclear weapons wrought shook the foundations of human existence....
>
> The dropping of the nuclear weapons is a problem that must be addressed globally. History is written by the victors. Thus, the heinous massacre that was Hiroshima has been handed down to us as a perfectly justified act of war.
>
> As a result, for over 50 years we have never directly confronted the full implications of this horrifying act for the future of the human race. Hence, we are still forced to live under the enormous threat of nuclear weapons....
>
> Beneath the atomic bomb's monstrous mushroom cloud, human skin was burned raw. Crying for water, human beings died in desperate agony. With thoughts of these victims as the starting point, it is incumbent upon us to think about the nuclear age and the relationship between human beings and nuclear weapons....
>
> The unique characteristic of the atomic bombing was that the enormous destruction was instantaneous and universal. Old, young, male, female, soldier, civilian – the killing was utterly indiscriminate. The entire city was exposed to the compound and devastating effects of thermal rays, shock wave blast, and radiation....
>
> Above all, we must focus on the fact that the human misery caused by the atomic bomb is different from that caused by conventional weapons. [H]uman bodies were burned by the thermal rays and high-temperature fires, broken and lacerated by the blast, and insidiously attacked by radiation. These forms of dam-

age compounded and amplified each other, and the name given to the combination was "A-bomb disease...."

[T]he bomb reduced Hiroshima to an inhuman state utterly beyond human ability to express or imagine. I feel frustrated at not being able to express this completely in my testimony about the tragedy of the atomic bombing....

It is clear that the use of nuclear weapons, which cause indiscriminate mass murder that leaves survivors to suffer for decades, is a violation of international law.[10]

Both Hiraoka and Iccho Ito, Mayor of Nagasaki, repeated to the Court the accounts of survivors. Thus Ito testified:

A 14-year old boy exposed to the atomic bombing two kilometers from the hypocenter described his experience as follows: "The air-raid shelter in Sakamoto-machi was filled with the dead and injured. The area near the shelter was strewn with corpses, some scorched black and others half-naked with puffed-up faces and skin hanging off like rags. It filled me with sorrow to see, among these, the corpses a mother clinging to her newborn baby and her three other children lying dead nearby. I could do nothing for the people screaming for help from under the ruins of houses or the people crawling along the ground dragging their burnt skin and begging for water. These screams of agony in the throes of death echoed in the ruins all night. When my father found a pot in the ruins and used it to draw water from a stream, the injured drank it greedily but then lay down and died on the ground. The following morning the screams had subsided, leaving only a world of death like a hell on Earth." This boy's four-year old sister died on August 10, and his mother, who had suffered severe burns, died on August 17. Then, 12 years later, his father died of stomach cancer.[11]

Ito concluded:

It is my ardent hope that, in its review, this Court will decide impartially about the inhumanity of nuclear weapons and their illegality in view of international law and in that way bring strength and hope, not only to the citizens of Nagasaki and Hiroshima, but to all the peace-loving people of the world. This indeed will contribute more than anything else to the repose of the souls of the 214,000 people who perished in the atomic wastelands of Nagasaki and Hiroshima 50 years ago.[12]

For the Marshall Islands, Lijon Eknilang of the Rongelap Atoll local government described the effects of her community's exposure to radiation from the United States' "Bravo" atmospheric nuclear test explosion. She told the Court:

> Mr. President, Members of the Court, I would like to begin by thanking you for allowing me to present a statement on the effects which the explosion of nuclear weapons have had on my life and on the lives of my family, friends, and other fellow citizens of the Marshall Islands. These experiences are relevant to the questions put to this Court, because unnecessary injuries, indiscriminate impacts, and adverse collateral environmental effects of the radioactive fall-out resulting from atmospheric tests which have so gravely affected the Marshall Islands would be repeated for other people and their lands in the event of any military use of nuclear weapons....
>
> On the morning of 1 March 1954, the day of the "Bravo" shot, there was a huge, brilliant light that consumed the sky. We all ran outside our home to see it. The elders said another world war had begun. I remember crying. I did not realize at the time that it was the people of Rongelap who had begun a lifelong battle for their health and a safe environment. Not long after the light from Bravo, it began to snow in Rongelap. We had heard about snow from the missionaries and other westerners who had come to our islands, but this was the first time we saw white particles fall from the sky and cover our village. Of course, in 1954, Marshallese children and their parents did not know that the snow was radioactive fall-out from the Bravo shot....
>
> Women have experienced many reproductive cancers and abnormal births. Marshallese women suffer silently and differently from the men who were exposed to radiation. Our culture and religion teaches us that reproductive abnormalities are a sign that women have been unfaithful to their husbands. For this reason, many of my friends keep quiet about the strange births they had. In privacy, they give birth, not to children as we like to think of them, but to things we could only describe as "octopuses," "apples," "turtles," and other things in our experience. We do not have Marshallese words for these kinds of babies because they were never born before the radiation came.... The most common birth defects on Rongelap and nearby islands have been "jellyfish" babies. These babies are born with no bones in their bodies and with transparent skin. We can see their brains and hearts beating. The babies usually live for a day or two before they stop breathing. Many women die from abnormal preg-

nancies and those who survive give birth to what looks like purple grapes which we quickly hide away and bury.[13]

The nuclear weapon states had little to say regarding the effects of nuclear weapons. The United States briefly responded in an abstract manner, making no reference to its bombings of Hiroshima and Nagasaki or its nuclear test explosions in the Marshall Islands. John McNeill, Senior Deputy General Counsel, Department of Defense, told the Court:

> The World Health Organization and some States have submitted to the Court materials discussing the destructive effects of nuclear weapons, including the effect of their use on human health and the environment. It is true that the use of nuclear weapons would have an adverse collateral effect on human health and both the natural and physical environment. But so too can the use of conventional weapons. Obviously, World Wars I and II, as well as the 1990-1991 conflict resulting from Iraq's invasion of Kuwait, dramatically demonstrated that conventional war can inflict terrible collateral damage to the environment. The fact is that armed conflict of any kind can cause widespread, sustained destruction; the Court need not examine scientific evidence to take judicial notice of this evident truth.
>
> Some States have adverted to studies of the effects of nuclear weapons in an attempt to demonstrate that every use of every type of nuclear weapon would necessarily violate principles of proportionality and discriminate use. But the material that has been presented for the Court's consideration cannot support such a sweeping proposition. Any given study rests on static assumptions: assumptions regarding the yield of a weapon, the technology that occasions how much radiation the weapon may release, where, in relation to the earth's surface it will be detonated, and the military objective at which it would be targeted.
>
> The assumptions made by the World Health Organization in the materials submitted to the Court are in fact highly selective (*Effects of Nuclear War on Health and Health Services*, 2nd ed., 1987). The four scenarios on which the World Health Organization Report focuses address civilian casualties expected to result from nuclear attacks involving significant number of large urban area targets or a substantial number of military targets. But no reference is made in the report to the effects to be expected from other plausible scenarios, such as a small number of accurate attacks by low-yield weapons against an equally small number of military targets in non-urban areas. The plausibility of such sce-

narios follows from a fact noted in the WHO Report by Professor Rotblat: namely, that "remarkable improvements" in the performance of nuclear weapons in recent years have resulted in their "much greater accuracy" (J. Rotblat, p. 95). Clearly, such possible scenarios would not necessarily raise issues of proportionality or discrimination.[14]

Humanitarian Law

Humanitarian law consists of rules and principles that regulate the conduct of warfare, seeking to strike a balance between the imperatives of war and the humanitarian impulse to moderate its savagery. Also known as the law of war or the law of armed conflict, it is codified in several important multilateral treaties, the Hague Conventions of 1907, the 1949 Geneva Conventions, the 1977 First Additional Protocol to the Geneva Conventions, and in other international instruments. Humanitarian law is widely acknowledged to be customary international law binding on states not parties to the relevant treaties. Customary international law is conventionally defined as based upon the general and consistent practice of states, followed out of a sense of legal obligation, but some customary rules also reflect underlying moral consideration.

The 1907 Hague Conventions represent the first systematic treaty codification of humanitarian rules. While the Hague Conventions did not adequately anticipate military techniques employed in the two world wars, notably "strategic" bombing of cities, they did express basic purposes of humanitarian law to set limits on warfare and protect non-combatant persons and property. Article 22 provided that "the right of belligerents to adopt means of injuring the enemy is not unlimited;" Article 23 prohibited the employment of poisoned weapons and weapons calculated to cause unnecessary suffering; Article 25 prohibited bombing of undefended cities; Article 27 enjoined protection "so far as possible" of buildings devoted to cultural and medical purposes. The 1949 Geneva Conventions mainly aim at protecting prisoners of war, the wounded and sick, the shipwrecked, and civilians in occupied territories (*e.g.*, after successful invasion of enemy territory). The 1977 Protocol I to the Geneva Conventions comprehensively codifies humanitarian law in light of the terrible experiences of 20th century warfare, providing detailed and strict protection of civilians from the effects of warfare. It represents in good measure the world's unambiguous repudiation of World War II strategic bombing. Unlike the older multilateral treaties, Protocol I has not yet been ratified by several major states, but most of its key provisions are acknowledged to state binding customary law.

Humanitarian law centrally involves two of the principles described by New Zealand, that states must distinguish between civilian personnel and objects and military targets, and that they may not employ methods and means of warfare that inflict unnecessary suffering, and is founded upon "elementary considerations of humanity" and the "dictates of the public conscience." Because humanitarian law applies to nuclear weapons just as it does to any weapon, explained Egypt's advocate, Professor George Abi-Saad, there is no need for a prohibition specific to nuclear weapons:

> [T]he use of nuclear weapons is prohibited not because they are or they are called nuclear weapons. They fall under the prohibitions of the fundamental and mandatory rules of humanitarian law which long predate them, *by their effects*; not because they are nuclear weapons, but because they are indiscriminate weapons of mass destruction.[15]

As its written statement, Sweden submitted a report approved by its parliament relying principally on the requirement of discrimination between military targets and civilian population or property in support of a conclusion of illegality.[16]

Faced with a powerful case based on humanitarian law and the world's experience with nuclear explosions and radiation, the nuclear weapon states were not reticent about defending the possible use of nuclear weapons. The United States, the United Kingdom, and the Russian Federation generally acknowledged that nuclear weapons, like all weapons, are subject to humanitarian law, whether used in a war of aggression or self-defence. "Restrictions set by the rules applicable to armed conflicts in respect of means and methods of warfare definitely also extend to nuclear weapons," said A.G. Khodakov, Director, Legal Department, Ministry of Foreign Affairs, Russian Federation.[17] For the United States, McNeill stated, "The United States has long shared the view that the law of armed conflict governs the use of nuclear weapons – just as it governs the use of conventional weapons."[18]

But the weapon states argued that humanitarian law only operates to restrict, not to prohibit, the use of nuclear weapons. The legality of use, the United States, United Kingdom, and Russia claimed, depends upon the circumstances of each case and cannot be prejudged. The United States' McNeill stated, "Under the law of armed conflict, in the absence of an express prohibition, the legality of the use of any weapon, including nuclear weapons, is fundamentally dependent on the facts and circumstances of the use in question."[19] Unlike the other participating weapon states, France, perhaps considering discretion the better part of valor, chose not to analyze the application of humanitarian law to use of nuclear weapons, emphasizing rather its right to use such weapons in self-defence absent an express prohibition. However, France did not contest that there are humanitarian constraints on such use.

Indiscriminate harm and unnecessary suffering

The prohibition of inflicting indiscriminate harm, universally accepted as binding law, and set forth in its modern form in Protocol I, was summarized by British Attorney General Nicholas Lyell (paralleling New Zealand's statement) as follows:

> *first*, it is unlawful to direct an attack against the civilian population or civilian objects as such; only military objectives are legitimate targets of attack; and
>
> *second*, even a military target must not be attacked if to do so would cause collateral civilian casualties or damage to civilian property which is excessive in relation to the concrete and direct military advantage anticipated from the attack, an aspect of the wider principle of proportionality...[20]

Lyell then argued that nuclear weapons can be discriminately targeted against military objectives, and that collateral civilian casualties can be acceptable *if the military gain is sufficiently great*:

> We fully accept that these principles operate as a constraint on the use of nuclear weapons – and all other weapons. But it is a fallacy to argue that *every* use of a nuclear weapon *must* contravene those principles.... It is possible to direct [nuclear weapons] quite precisely against military objectives and thus to comply with the first principle.... Nor is it to be assumed that the use of a nuclear weapon against a military objective will inevitably cause disproportionate civilian casualties.... *[T]he greater the military advantage which can be reasonably expected ... the greater the risk of collateral civilian casualties which may have to be regarded as within the law*. Where what is at stake is the difference between national survival and subjection to conquest which may be of the most brutal and enslaving character, it is dangerously wrong to say that the use of a nuclear weapon could never meet the criterion of proportionality.[21]

Similarly, McNeill argued for the United States that whether "incidental injury" to civilians is permissible would depend on the military necessity of the attack, stating:

> [I]t is not possible in the abstract, without knowledge of the precise circumstances of particular uses of nuclear weapons, to determine that such uses would be violative of [humanitarian law]. Nuclear weapons, as is true of conventional weapons, can be used in a variety of ways: they can be deployed to achieve a wide

range of military objectives of varying degrees of significance; they can be targeted in ways that either increase or decrease resulting incidental civilian injury or collateral damage; and their use may be lawful or not depending upon whether and to what extent such use was prompted by another belligerent's conduct and the nature of such conduct.... Modern nuclear weapon delivery systems are, indeed, capable of precisely engaging discrete military objectives.... *Whether the use of nuclear weapons in any given instance would result in the infliction of disproportionate collateral destruction or incidental injury to civilians cannot be judged in the abstract. Such a judgment depends entirely on the circumstances of the contemplated use, including the military necessity of destroying a particular objective.*[22]

The weapon states again argued that military factors must be weighed in determining whether the prohibition of causing unnecessary suffering is violated. Russia's Khodakov relied on the International Committee of the Red Cross (ICRC), a recognized authority because of its role in developing humanitarian law, citing its statement that "the concept of 'unnecessary' suffering would seem to call for correlation between the military advantages of any given weapon and humanitarian considerations."[23] He concluded that the prohibition "is not in itself a general ban on the use of nuclear weapons *per se.*"[24]

The non-nuclear weapon states rejected the claim that nuclear weapons can be used discriminately. Also invoking the Red Cross, but to different effect, was Costa Rica's representative, Dr. Carlos Vargas Pizarro. He quoted the following portion of an analysis prepared for the Court by the ICRC:

> [N]o one can be unaware of the fact that today nuclear arms of all kinds are generally considered to be weapons of mass destruction, as are biological and chemical weapons. *A priori*, their use would thus appear to be incompatible with the prohibition, reaffirmed in Protocol I, of methods or means of combat which cannot be directed at a specific military objective and thus of a nature to strike military objectives and civilians, without distinction.[25]

Also rejected was the claim that the extent of legally acceptable civilian death and injury arising from a nuclear attack is dependent upon the attack's military justification, an approach that could validate a wide range of uses of nuclear weapons, notably against an enemy's nuclear forces. In rebuttal, Zimbabwe's representative, Jonathan Wutawunashe, again citing the Red Cross analysis, stated:

> The United Kingdom ... stretched the military necessity argument when it claimed that, if a large military *advantage* were at stake, high civilian losses and damages may be justified. The Red Cross ... categorically opposed this argument, stating that Protocol I "does not provide any justification for attacks which cause extensive civilian losses and damages. Incidental losses and damages should never be extensive." ... Even before 1977, it was a universally recognized principle of humanitarian law that mass slaughter of civilians is illegal no matter the provocation or military advantage which may be gained.[26]

On behalf of the Marshall Islands, a principal site for atmospheric nuclear tests carried out by the United States, Theodore Kronmiller stated:

> The experience of the Marshallese people confirms that unnecessary suffering is an unavoidable consequence of the detonation of nuclear weapons, even at great distances from human populations.... [H]uman populations which are hundreds, or even thousands, of miles from a nuclear blast may be caused to suffer serious injury, death after prolonged illness and severe birth defects.... We also conclude, from the great extent of human injury and environmental and property damage inflicted on the Marshall Islands by nuclear weapons detonations, that these devices are inherently indiscriminate in their effects.... The radioactive contaminations of islands far distant from the test sites resulted in the long-term, and perhaps permanent, loss of productive resources and family dwellings...[27]

General principles of humanity and the Martens Clause
In addition to the prohibitions of inflicting indiscriminate and unnecessary harm, several non-nuclear weapon states urged the relevance of general principles of humanity, elementary considerations of humanity, and dictates of the public conscience, underlying those prohibitions. Along with treaties and customs, Article 38 of the Statute of the International Court of Justice lists as a basis for the Court's decisions and opinions "the general principles of law recognized by civilized nations."[28] The Martens Clause, named after Russian foreign minister Feodoro de Martens, is set forth in the Hague Conventions and in the Geneva Conventions and Protocols. As stated in Geneva Protocol I, it provides:

> In cases not covered by this protocol or by other international agreements, civilians and combatants remain under the protection and authority of the principles of international law derived

from established custom, from *principles of humanity* and from the *dictates of public conscience*. (Emphasis added.)

Australia's Minister of Foreign Affairs Gareth Evans told the Court:

> We submit that the principles of international law of most direct and obvious relevance to the legality of nuclear weapons are the general principles of humanitarian law. The existence of "fundamental general principles of humanitarian law," against which the conduct of States can be judged under customary international law, was recognized by this Court in *the Military and Paramilitary Activities* case [Nicaragua versus United States]. These "principles of humanitarian law" were also recognized in the *Corfu Channel* case, in which the Court referred to "certain general and well-recognized principles, namely: elementary considerations of humanity...." The general principles may in some respects be broader than any existing treaty provision, and may apply in situations where there is no applicable treaty provision at all.
>
> This is specifically recognized in the so-called "Martens clauses" in some of the humanitarian conventions....
>
> Of course, neither the concept of "humanity," nor the "dictates of public conscience" are static. Conduct which might have been considered acceptable by the international community earlier this century might be condemned as inhumane by the international community today.
>
> ... It is not to the point that it may be possible to conceive of theoretical situations in which a nuclear weapon may cause no more damage than certain conventional weapons. The fact remains that the existence of nuclear weapons as a class of weapons threatens the whole of civilization. This is not the case with respect to any class or classes of conventional weapons. It cannot be consistent with humanity to permit the existence of a weapon which threatens the very survival of humanity. The threat of global annihilation engendered by the existence of such weapons, and the fear that this has engendered amongst the entire post-war generation, is itself an evil, as much as nuclear war itself. If not always at the forefront of our everyday thinking, the shadow of the mushroom cloud remains in all our minds. It has pervaded our thoughts about the future, about our children, about human nature. And it has pervaded the thoughts of our children themselves, who are deeply anxious about their future in a world where nuclear weapons remain.[29]

Zimbabwe, Mexico, Iran, Costa Rica, Malaysia, Samoa and other non-nuclear weapon states drew particular attention to one of the elements mentioned by Australia, the "dictates of the public conscience" identified by the Martens Clause. For Zimbabwe, Jonathan Wutawunashe noted that millions of declarations of public conscience from individuals of both nuclear and non-nuclear countries, stating their conviction that nuclear weapons are immoral and therefore illegal, had been presented to the Court.[30] (Their acceptance by the Court's registrar was a first.)

On behalf of Mexico, Under Secretary of Foreign Relations Sergio Gonzalez Galvez cited the Martens clause and stated:

> And if there any doubts concerning the preoccupation of mankind regarding this problem, the association of survivors of the nuclear attacks against Nagasaki and Hiroshima handed me in New York the copies of 100,000 signatures, out of the 50 million persons who subscribed a declaration expressing their repudiation of nuclear weapons.[31]

For Iran, Javad Zarif cited General Assembly resolutions under the heading of dictates of the public conscience as evidence of abhorrence of the use of nuclear weapons and of the illegality of such use.[32]

For Costa Rica, Vargas Pizarro stated:

> With respect to the public conscience, Costa Rica wishes to draw the Court's attention to the position adopted by the Federation of American Scientists, which was founded in 1945 by atomic scientists who had participated in the Manhattan Project. They declare that: "The use of any weapon of mass destruction such as chemical, biological or nuclear is, and ought to be declared, illegal under international law."[33]

For Malaysia, Attorney General Dato' Mohtar Abdullah stated:

> In the context of nuclear weapons the so-called proportionality and necessity principles cannot apply at all. If a weapon is inherently in violation of the Martens Clause, that is, if it is a weapon incompatible with the laws of humanity and the dictates of the public conscience, its use cannot be justified on grounds of proportionality, military necessity, self-defence, reprisal, deterrence, or any other principle.[34]

On behalf of Samoa, Professor Roger Clark raised crimes against humanity in connection with the Martens Clause and general principles. General Assembly resolution 1653 declares that the use of nuclear weapons is "a direct violation of the [United Nations] Charter" and "contrary to the rules of international law and to the laws of humanity," and a state using them is "to be considered as acting contrary to the laws of humanity and as committing a crime against mankind and civilization." Clark observed regarding resolution 1653, "The echoes of the Martens Clause here are loud and clear."[35] Clark also told the Court:

> The concept of crimes against humanity was treated in the Nuremberg process, in which it was crystallized, as based on general principles of municipal law, although it also harks back to Martens. In more recent usage, in connection with prosecutions in the former Yugoslavia and Rwanda, it has connotations both of humanitarian law and of human rights law. It thus seems to be exactly the right concept to describe the use of nuclear weaponry, whether in international or in non-international conflict.[36]

The United States attempted to dismiss the Martens Clause by arguing that it clarifies only that in the absence of a specific treaty provision, a means of warfare remains subject to general rules of customary international law. According to McNeill, the clause does not "transform public opinion into rules of customary international law."[37] The United Kingdom argued that "a new rule of customary law cannot, contrary to what has been claimed, be derived simply from general humanitarian principles."[38] The cases in which general principles were cited by the Court, *Corfu Channel* and *Military and Paramilitary Activities*, Lyell maintained, simply found a legal obligation to notify shippers of known minefields, "a far cry indeed from the proposed outlawing *per se* of a lawful weapon."[39]

The arguments of the United Kingdom and the United States sought to collapse non-treaty international law into customary law reflecting state practice, ignoring that there are sources of international law other than treaty and custom. This approach was challenged by the Solomon Islands' advocate, Professor James Crawford. He told the Court, "Neither general principles of law nor general considerations of humanity have to be consented to before they bind *all* States."[40]

Environmental Law

The prohibition of causing severe damage to the environment

Protocol I to the Geneva Conventions, Article 35(3), prohibits the use of methods or means of warfare which are intended or may be expected to cause widespread, long-term and severe damage to the natural environment. The Convention on the Prohibition of Military or any other Hostile Use of Environmental Modification Techniques prohibits the use of modification techniques having widespread, long-lasting or severe effects. Also, as Iran's Javad Zarif observed, long established rules of the law of war that generally protect the environment include "proportionality and the prohibition on military operations not directed against legitimate military targets, as well as the prohibition of destruction of enemy property not imperatively demanded by the necessities of war."[41]

The nuclear weapon states disputed the applicability of Article 35 of Protocol I and the Environmental Modification Convention. The latter was opposed on the ground that use of nuclear weapons would not necessarily involve the "deliberate manipulation" of natural processes comparable, for example, to weather modification. Concerning Protocol I, the weapons states denied that its prohibition of causing severe damage to the natural environment, as well as its prohibition of reprisals against civilians, are binding with respect to nuclear weapons. These were not simply restatements of rules previously acknowledged to be binding with respect to all weapons, they argued, but rather enactment of new rules that were understood not to apply to nuclear weapons. In support of this position, they cited a statement of the Red Cross that "prohibitions relating to atomic, bacteriological and chemical weapons are subjects of international agreements or negotiations by governments, and in submitting these draft Additional Protocols the ICRC does not intend to broach these problems."[42] They also cited declarations made by the United States, the United Kingdom, and France made at the outset and close of the negotiations.

According to Britain's Lyell, the "nuclear understanding"

> meant, first, that there would be no attempt to make specific provisions for nuclear weapons in the text, and no such provisions were made. Secondly, it meant that any new provisions in-

troduced into the law of armed conflict by the Additional Protocols would apply only to conventional weapons.

We fully accept, however, that the use of nuclear weapons is subject to the principles of customary international law, and it is plain that some of the provisions of Additional Protocol I did no more than reaffirm and codify principles of the customary law of armed conflict which already existed and which apply to the use of all weapons, including nuclear weapons. But it is equally plain that other provisions of the Protocol, such as those on the environment and those on reprisals, were understood to be new rules.[43]

The non-weapon states replied that specific regulations or prohibitions of *any* category of weapon were not the subject of negotiation; such negotiations were to be carried out elsewhere. Rather, they stated, the Protocol contains general rules applying to all categories of weapons. Concerning the alleged "nuclear understanding," Abi-Saad stated for Egypt:

Now this "understanding" took the form of interpretative declarations which could not have been objected to. Still several other States made differing, contradictory, interpretative declarations, thus refuting the contention that the Conference had accepted the nuclear powers' understanding or acquiesced to it; a contention which stretches too far the significance of the decision of the Conference not to deal specifically with weapons, leaving the subject to other fora where negotiations on prohibitions *per se* were in process or about to begin.

[W]hat was excluded from the ambit of the Conference and the Protocols was the specific treatment of arms, including nuclear weapons, and not the applicability of the general rules to them as well as to all other weapons past and future. This comes out clearly from an obviously objective source, it is the *Commentary* of the International Committee of the Red Cross on the Protocols, where it is stated: "delegations agreed not to discuss nuclear weapons. But it cannot be inferred from that the rules of Protocol I do not apply to nuclear weapons ..."[44]

Abi-Saad also argued that the Protocol I prohibition of inflicting severe damage on the environment as a means of warfare "is innovative, but only in specifying the application of the general rules to modern means and methods of warfare, not in the normative composition itself."[45]

General environmental law

To support the applicability of the Protocol I prohibition, and to argue more broadly for the existence of a binding customary law principle of environmental security applicable both in peace and war, several states cited declarations of international conferences. Thus Iran's Javad Zarif referred to Principle 24 of the Rio Declaration on Environment and Development:

> Warfare is inherently destructive of sustainable development. States shall therefore respect international law providing protection for the environment in times of armed conflict and cooperate in its future development, as necessary.[46]

For the Solomon Islands, Philippe Sands cited Principle 21 of the Stockholm Declaration, reaffirmed in Principle 2 of the Rio Declaration, which requires states "to ensure that activities within their jurisdiction or control do not cause damage to the environment of other states or of areas beyond the limits of national jurisdiction."[47] Also cited in support of a principle of environmental security were treaties enjoining care and preservation of the environment beyond a nation's jurisdiction, for example the Biodiversity Convention, the Climate Change Convention, the Law of the Sea Convention, and the Vienna Convention on the Protection of the Ozone Layer.[48]

In its written submission concerning the World Health Assembly question, Ukraine stated:

> Ukraine as a state which suffered the ruinous and disastrous consequences of Chernobyl nuclear catastrophe and voluntarily declared its intention to become a non nuclear state in the future is deeply convinced that in view of the health and environmental effects the use of nuclear weapons by a State in War or other armed conflict would be a breach of its obligations under international law including the WHO Constitution.[49]

Though noting that international environmental law is in the process of development, the nuclear weapons states disputed that any customary principle of environmental security applicable in time of war has crystallized. Marc Perrin de Brichambaut of the French Ministry of Foreign Affairs stated regarding the Rio and Stockholm declarations that "these documents, apart from the fact that they clearly have no binding force, do not in any way bear on the legality of nuclear weapons."[50] Concerning environmental treaties, the nuclear weapons states urged, as Lyell stated for the United Kingdom, that "[t]heir principal purpose is the protection of the environment in times of peace," and that it would be "destabilizing to the rule of law to see these treaties now interpreted in such a way as to prohibit the use of nuclear weapons."⁵¹ Lyell added that "it is dangerous nonsense to suggest that States which dealt so carefully with nuclear weapons in the context of the laws of war and disarmament would, almost casually, have accepted" such an interpretation.⁵²

The Solomon Islands' Sands commented:

> [T]hese are the same States which pride themselves – with some justification – on their role in promulgating the rule of law, promoting human rights and preserving the environment. Yet when it comes to those very weapons of mass destruction which pose a greater threat to human rights and the environment than anything else imaginable, these States ask you to set aside that body of principles and rules so carefully put in place over the past 50 years. They ask you, in effect, to re-situate yourself in 1945, to ignore all subsequent developments and to follow Balzac's dubious proposition, "that laws are spider webs through which the big flies pass and the little ones get caught."⁵³

Reprisals

An illegal use of nuclear weapons is permitted, the nuclear weapon states contended, in retaliation against another state's illegal use of nuclear weapons or other comparable illegal act. Under customary law, the United States specified in a written statement, reprisals "must be taken with the intent to cause the enemy to cease violations of the law of armed conflict, other means of securing compliance should be exhausted, and the reprisals must be proportionate to the violations."[54] The United States' McNeill told the Court:

> Even if it were to be concluded – as we clearly have not – that the use of nuclear weapons would necessarily be unlawful, the customary law of reprisal permits a belligerent to respond to another party's violation of the law of armed conflict by resorting to what otherwise would be unlawful conduct. Whether a use of force would or would not be lawful, and whether or not it would be justified as a reprisal, depends, obviously and necessarily, upon the circumstances surrounding the act in question. The law of reprisal does not and cannot, therefore, be construed as prohibiting categorically the use of nuclear weapons; indeed, if it were to be so construed, the negative implications for strategic deterrence would be obvious and dire.[55]

In a written statement, the Netherlands took a similar view:

> [E]ven if it were to be assumed that the (first) use of nuclear weapons by a State were unlawful *per se* under present international law – *quod non* -, this would not necessarily exclude the permissibility of the use of nuclear weapons by way of belligerent reprisal against an unlawful use of (nuclear) weapons, provided of course the retaliating State observed the conditions set by international law for the taking of lawful reprisals, *i.e.* satisfies, *inter alia*, the requirement that the retaliation is proportionate and serves as an *ultimum remedium*.[56]

The non-nuclear weapon states rejected this claim as wholly inconsistent with the thrust of humanitarian law towards protecting civilians against the effects of warfare. As Mexico's Gonzalez Galvez, told the Court: "Torture is not a permissible response to torture. Nor is mass rape acceptable retaliation for mass rape. Just as unacceptable is retaliatory deterrence – 'You have burnt my city, I will burn yours'."[57] In a written submission, Nauru argued that a nuclear reprisal is illegal because the notion of a proportionate response loses all meaning in the context of a nuclear exchange.[58] Professor Eric David stated on behalf of the Solomon Islands:

> [T]hough it may seem harsh to contend that a State which is the victim of a nuclear attack cannot respond with nuclear weapons, this is because, yet again, humanitarian law places the interests of the victims above the interests of States. If the dispatch of a nuclear weapon causes a million deaths, retaliation with another nuclear weapon which will also cause a million deaths will perhaps protect the sovereignty of the State suffering the first strike, and will perhaps satisfy the victims' desire for revenge, but it will not satisfy humanitarian law, which will have been breached not once but twice; and two wrongs do not make a right.[59]

In particular, the non-weapon states noted, reprisals are contrary to the express provisions of Protocol I to the Geneva Conventions. Protocol I contains a comprehensive set of prohibitions of reprisals, including reprisals against civilian populations and objects indispensable to the survival of the civilian population (*e.g.*, foodstuffs, drinking water installations). In a written submission, the Solomon Islands also stated that protection of civilians bars *any* reprisal with nuclear weapons, including against military targets or personnel, due to the "very nature of nuclear weapons (excluding virtually any possibility of limiting their effects to military targets and avoiding a total war)."[60]

Against the weapon states' argument that Protocol I's rules regarding reprisals are "new rules" understood not to apply to nuclear weapons, the non-weapons states maintained that humanitarian rules protecting civilians are long established *jus cogens* rules. *Jus cogens* or peremptory law is universally binding law that may not be violated or denied in any circumstance, including by the conclusion of treaties or other formal state action (for example, the declarations of nuclear weapon states concerning the scope of Protocol I). It can be compared to basic rules of a constitutional character that set the framework for all other law within a state. (In the advisory opinion, the Court declined to pass on the question of whether humanitarian rules have a *jus cogens* character, but did hold that they are "fundamental" and "intransgressible."[61])

Egypt's Abi-Saad told the Court that the prohibition of reprisals against civilians is an application of the "fundamental and peremptory" rule requiring parties to a conflict to discriminate between military objectives and civilians and not to attack civilians as such.[62] For the Solomon Islands, Crawford observed that the Protocol I rules regarding reprisals and the environment "are cognate with and are underpinned by the 'elementary considerations of humanity', 'the general principles of humanitarian law' to which this Court referred in a series of cases."[63] As they did with respect to the prohibition of causing severe damage to the environment, non-weapon states also argued that there was no agreement during negotiation of Protocol I that nuclear weapons would be exempted from the operation of its rules regarding reprisals; rather the only shared "understanding" was that categories of weapons as such were not the subject of negotiation.

The Law Of Neutrality

Article I of Hague Convention No. 5 provides that "the territory of neutral powers is inviolable." Many non-nuclear weapon states argued that fall-out from use of nuclear weapons would inevitably and significantly affect states not participating in the conflict in violation of their neutrality rights. Thus Javad Zarif of Iran told the Court that "use of nuclear weapons, due to their uncontrollable effects, constitute neutrality-violating devices *par excellence*."[64] The United States' written position was that the law of neutrality is understood to preclude military invasion or bombardment of neutrals, but has never been applied to collateral damage to neutral territory for lawful acts of war committed outside that territory.[65] The reply of the Solomon Islands was that *any* material effect is precluded by the terms of the Hague rule.[66] The United Kingdom and United States also maintained that whether use of nuclear weapons would cause damage in neutral states is speculative.[67] In this regard, Sands observed for the Solomon Islands:

> [S]ome States are frankly economical in their sense of reality.... [Health and environmental effects] would inevitably be felt in the target State, but they would also be felt in other States and in areas beyond national jurisdiction. Those effects would be widespread and they would be massive – this is the experience of Hiroshima and Nagasaki. It is also the experience of the atmospheric tests carried out in the Pacific region – as Mrs. Eknilang indicated this morning – and in North Africa, and it is confirmed scientific opinion. It is finally confirmed by the Chernobyl accident which led to widespread radioactive fall-out over most of Europe.[68]

Human Rights

International human rights instruments set forth the rights of persons that must be respected by states. They are most commonly invoked concerning the relations between a state and its citizens and other persons within its territory. In the course of the proceedings, however, several states contended that, in view of the extraordinary consequences of a nuclear explosion, reaching far beyond the site of hostilities in space and time, human rights law prohibits the use of nuclear weapons by one state against another because such use would violate the rights of persons both in the target state and in neutral states.

Article 3 of the Universal Declaration of Human rights, widely recognized as an authoritative statement of customary international law, provides: "Everyone has the right to life, liberty and security of person." Its article 25 provides: "Everyone has the right to a standard of living adequate for health and well-being ..." Article 6 of the International Covenant on Civil and Political Rights, a widely ratified treaty, provides: "Every human being has the inherent right to life. This right shall be protected by law. No one shall be arbitrarily deprived of his life." Article 4 of the treaty provides that the right to life is not among those rights subject to derogation, *i.e.* non-compliance by a state, in time of public emergency. Article 12(1) of the International Covenant on Economic, Social and Cultural Rights, also widely ratified, provides: "The States Parties to the present Covenant recognize the right of everyone to the enjoyment of the highest attainable standard of physical and mental health."

These and similar provisions were the basis for arguments made by the Solomon Islands, Costa Rica, and other states. In its written submissions, the Solomon Islands linked the right to health, the right to life, and international environmental law, arguing that the use of nuclear weapons would violate rules requiring protection of human health and the environment.[69] Similarly, Costa Rica's Vargas Pizarro told the Court:

> [A]ny use or threat of nuclear weapons by a State would violate the international law obligations reflected under the rules for the protection of the human right to life, health, a clean and healthy environment, and peace; and especially the universality, indivisibility and interdependency of those rights.... [N]uclear threat

or use cannot coexist with the achievement of a global order embodying common security that realizes the purposes of the United Nations and provides fundamental human rights for all persons...[70]

Malaysia, Indonesia, and other states also drew the Court's attention to a general comment made by the United Nations Human Rights Committee, which supervises the implementation of the International Covenant on Civil and Political Rights.[71] The Committee found that:

> It is evident that the designing, testing, manufacture, possession and deployment of nuclear weapons are among the greatest threats to the right to life which confront mankind today. This threat is compounded by the danger that the actual use of such weapons may be brought about, not only in the event of war, but even through human or mechanical error or failure.
>
> Furthermore, the very existence and gravity of this threat generate a climate of suspicion and fear between States, which is in itself antagonistic to the promotion of universal respect for and observance of human rights and fundamental freedoms in accordance with the Charter of the United Nations and the International Covenants on Human Rights.
>
> The production, testing, possession, deployment and use of nuclear weapons should be prohibited and recognized as crimes against humanity.[72]

The response of the nuclear weapons states was that human rights treaties, in the words of Russia's Khodakov, "exist in a quite different dimension."[73] Perrin de Brichambaut stated for France that human rights instruments "do not recognize the right to life as being an absolute right. In particular, they do not provide any guarantee against threats to life as a result of legal acts of war."[74] For the United Kingdom, Lyell argued:

> [T]he right to life is not absolute. The prohibition – to draw on the International Covenant on Civil and Political Rights – is in respect of the *arbitrary* deprivation of life. In so far as this applies in armed conflict at all, it can only mean deprivation of life which is contrary to the laws of war. The reference to human rights treaties thus adds nothing, for the legality of a use of nuclear weapons continues to turn on the laws of war.[75]

The rejoinder of Sands for the Solomon Islands was that since any use of a nuclear weapon would violate humanitarian law, it "must necessarily also violate the right to life of those persons situated in the target State."⁷⁶ Further,

> even if it could be maintained that the use of a nuclear weapon was lawful against a target State, which Solomon Islands denies is ever the case, its effects on third States and areas beyond national jurisdiction can leave little doubt that principles of neutrality would inevitably be violated. Mrs. Eknilang's testimony makes it painfully clear that such effects would also violate the human rights of civilians at great distances from nuclear explosions in time and in place.⁷⁷

The Prohibition of Poisonous and Analogous Weapons

The Geneva Gas Protocol of 1925 prohibits the use in war of "asphyxiating, poisonous or other gases and of all analogous liquids, materials or devices." The Hague Regulations, Article 23(a), prohibit the use of poison or poisoned weapons. Many states argued that these provisions prohibit the use of nuclear weapons because of their radiation effects. For Qatar, Minister of Justice Najeeb Al-Nauimi stated that "there is no basis to make a distinction between the physical properties of poisonous gas and the physical properties of radiation as aptly illustrated by the radiation-enhanced neutron bomb."[78] He noted that radioactivity has

> an effect on living organisms [that] is similar to that of genotoxic poison and causes long term genetic risks even for those who are not directly involved in the conflict, including the children of those who are directly exposed.... With the mention of genetic risks I cannot help but stress the importance of the question before the Court for future generations.[79]

Al-Nauimi also observed that humanitarian law "should always be interpreted to give the benefit of the doubt in favour of the protection of the victim."[80]

The United Kingdom responded that the Geneva Gas Protocol and other international agreements prohibiting chemical weapons and biological and toxin weapons have never been understood by the ratifying states to apply to nuclear weapons. Lyell averred that the Protocol "was intended to apply to weapons the *primary* effects of which were poisonous ... whereas, the primary effects of nuclear weapons are devastating heat and blast."[81]

Replying for the Solomon Islands, David quoted a statement in the 1990 report of the U.N. Secretary General on nuclear weapons that "the most specific medical effects related to a nuclear explosion are the radiation injuries."[82] He further stated:

> The fact that nuclear weapons produce blast and heat does not justify their also producing radiation, whose effects are not only

typical of a nuclear reaction – which is precisely what likens the nuclear weapon to a chemical weapon and a poison weapon – but may, moreover, be felt far beyond the threatre of war and the period of the war itself.[83]

The Prohibition Of Genocide

The 1948 Genocide Convention prohibits killing and other acts intended to destroy, in whole or in part, a national, ethnical, racial or religious group, as such. Some states argued that use of nuclear weapons falls under this prohibition. The Solomon Islands explained in a written submission that a "large scale" use of nuclear weapons leading to the destruction of such a group would be genocide because the objective and foreseeable consequences of the use would establish intent.[84] "In light of the atrocities and malevolence that the history of this century associates with genocide," responded McNeill,

> the United States regrets that assertions of genocidal conduct have been so imprecisely made in this context.... [N]uclear weapons could be an instrument of genocide in the hands of a party harbouring the requisite *animus*, just as other weapons could be put to such unconscionable uses; but the fact of this potential would not, without more, render the use of nuclear weapons violative of the law against genocide.[85]

General Assembly Resolutions and the Nuclear Non-Proliferation Treaty

Many non-nuclear weapon states sought to establish the emergence of a specific customary prohibition of nuclear weapons, based on scores of General Assembly resolutions over three decades condemning use of nuclear weapons, the practice of non-use of the weapons since the United States' atomic bombings of Hiroshima and Nagasaki, and the illegality of possession or use of nuclear weapons in most of the world under the Nuclear Non-Proliferation Treaty, regional nuclear free zones, and negative security assurances committing nuclear weapons states not to use the weapons against non-possessing states.

General Assembly resolutions

The non-nuclear weapon states contended that the series of General Assembly resolutions beginning with resolution 1653, adopted in 1961 and finding the use of nuclear weapons to violate the United Nations Charter, the rules of international law, and the laws of humanity, represent an authoritative determination that use of nuclear weapons is illegal under existing general law. They also urged that the resolutions, together with the NPT and other developments, evidence the emergence of a rule of customary law specifically prohibiting such use.

For Malaysia, Dato' Mohtar argued that the resolutions "represent State practice in the interpretation of the laws of war [and] provide proof of international community standards and commitments."[86]

For Mexico, Gonzalez Galvez argued the relevance of the series of resolutions as tending to establish the existence of a specific customary prohibition, and in any case disproving any acceptance of the legality of the weapons. He explained that General Assembly resolutions,

> though lacking the binding force of a treaty, often express a general consensus – especially if they have been approved by a strong majority – and therefore they confirm or reinforce precedents in international law…. [Resolutions] are used as the best way of determining the principles recognized by nations, in my opinion not only to confirm the existence of a customary rule, but

to validate the theory of *lex ferenda* [developing law].... Finally, there is a decisive argument: whatever opinion one may have about the resolutions of a forum like the United Nations General Assembly, no one can claim that the opposite of what has been passed by an overwhelming majority in a forum that represents the feelings of almost all the nations in the world can be held as an international custom or as a generally recognized principle of international law.[87]

In response, the nuclear weapons states stressed that they and allied states have consistently opposed or abstained from voting on the General Assembly resolutions. "This fact," stated Lyell for the United Kingdom, "fatally undermines any notion that the resolutions express an *opinio juris* in favor of a prohibitive rule."[88] On behalf of France, Perrin de Brichambaut contended that "[i]t is universally accepted that the resolutions of the General Assembly have no binding force..."[89] Further,

> If it were shown that all the States forming that majority intended to create such a rule and not, as is most usually the case, to express a political point of view, it would suffice if some States objected – a situation which cannot be treated as insignificant, particularly since the objection is not confined to the nuclear-weapon States.[90]

Clark replied for Samoa:

> A large majority of the General Assembly insists that existing law applies. The nuclear States seek to opt out. Who must prove what? [T]he issue is whether the nuclear States have been able to establish for themselves special rules excluding the application of the general and pre-existing obligations of the law of armed conflict.[91]

For Costa Rica, Vargas Pizarro observed:

> Where matters fundamental to humanity are concerned, dissent cannot be permitted to prevent the emergence of a customary rule. An example of a non-consenting State not being exempted from a customary rule is South Africa, which persistently dissented from the rule prohibiting racial discrimination while that rule was developing.[92]

The Nuclear Non-Proliferation Treaty, regional nuclear weapon free zones, and other agreements and commitments

The Nuclear Non-Proliferation Treaty (NPT) entered into force in 1970. As of 1995, only a few states were not parties to the treaty, including, however, the undeclared nuclear weapon states of India, Pakistan, and Israel. Article II of the treaty prohibits non-nuclear weapon states from acquiring the weapons. Article I prohibits nuclear weapon states from supplying the weapons to non-weapon states. Article IX defines "nuclear weapon states" as states which had manufactured and exploded a nuclear weapon prior to 1967, *i.e.* the United States, France, Russia, the United Kingdom, and China. Article VI provides: "Each of the Parties to the Treaty undertakes to pursue negotiations in good faith on effective measures relating to cessation of the nuclear arms race at an early date and to nuclear disarmament, and on a treaty on general and complete disarmament under strict and effective international control."

Several states, notably Australia and New Zealand, argued that, in conjunction with other developments, the NPT obligations have now become customary law, binding on all states, with the result that possession and threat or use of nuclear weapons are universally illegal. Australia's Evans told the Court:

> Obligations under the Nuclear Non-Proliferation Treaty may have been no more than treaty obligations at the time it was concluded. However, over the years, the number of States Parties to the Treaty has steadily risen. By 1992, when China and France acceded to it, all five acknowledged nuclear-weapon States were Parties to it. It now has 180 States Parties, the vast majority of all States in the world. At the Nuclear Non-Proliferation Treaty Review and Extension Conference held in May this year, the Treaty was extended indefinitely by the unanimous decision of the Conference of States Parties. In view of this widespread, indeed near universal, adherence to the Treaty; in view of the indefinite duration now of its provisions; and in view of all the other international activities and evidence (not least in the context of the hostile reaction world-wide to the continued weapons testing by France and China) manifesting the clearest conviction that nuclear weapons must ultimately be eradicated, Australia submits that Articles I and II of the Nuclear Non-Proliferation Treaty must now be regarded as reflective of customary international law….
>
> This prohibition under customary international law must apply equally to nuclear-weapon States and non-nuclear-weapon States. It is in the nature of rules of customary international law that they apply to all States alike. If humanity and the dictates of

conscience demand the prohibition of such weapons for some States, it must demand the same prohibition for all States. And following the end of the Cold War, there can no longer be, if there ever was, any practical imperative for treating nuclear-weapon States and non-nuclear-weapon States differently. True, the Nuclear Non-Proliferation Treaty does not state that it is illegal for the nuclear-weapon States to continue to acquire, possess, test, threaten or use nuclear weapons. Indeed, it seems to assume that they will do some or all of these things, at least for a period. However, it is also true that the Non-Proliferation Treaty confers no positive right on the nuclear-weapon States to continue to possess such weapons. Furthermore, the Treaty does point to the ultimate aim of the complete elimination of nuclear weapons through general and complete nuclear disarmament. That Treaty cannot be seen as a bar to the emergence of a rule of customary international law which would fill the gap, making the threat or use of nuclear weapons illegal for nuclear-weapon States in the same way as for non-nuclear-weapon States....

Mr. President, Members of the Court, having reached this conclusion that the acquisition, development, testing, possession, use or threat of use of nuclear weapons is contrary to international law, it follows that all States are under an obligation to take positive action to eliminate completely nuclear weapons from the world. To implement this obligation, States which do not possess such weapons cannot lawfully acquire them, and States which do possess such weapons cannot add to, improve or test them. States which possess nuclear weapons must be subject to an obligation to eliminate their existing weapons. They must within a reasonable timeframe take systematic action to eliminate completely all nuclear weapons in a manner which is safe, and does not damage the environment....

During this transitional phase of negotiated nuclear disarmament, the nuclear-weapon States remain under a legal obligation to continue to negotiate in good faith with other States, and otherwise to make every possible effort to achieve complete nuclear disarmament within a reasonable time-frame. Such a "duty to negotiate" under customary international law is not unprecedented. An analogous duty exists in customary international law relating to continental shelf delimitations between neighboring or opposite coastal States. In that context, this Court has referred to the existence of a "duty to negotiate with a view to reaching agreement, and to do so in good faith, with a genuine intention to achieve a positive result."

> [D]uring this transitional phase, all States, including the nuclear weapon States are prohibited by customary international law from engaging in any action inconsistent with this commitment. They cannot introduce new nuclear weapons. They cannot refine their existing stockpiles. They cannot engage in action intended to ensure maintenance of their nuclear arsenals indefinitely into the future.[93]

Similarly, New Zealand's East told the court that the NPT has "delegitimized" nuclear weapons by banning their acquisition by most states and committing the nuclear weapons states to their elimination. "The agreed premise of the treaty," he said, "is that a world free of nuclear weapons would be a better and more secure place." Further, "[t]he principle of nonproliferation, of the unacceptability, of nuclear weapons, is so widely accepted that it can now be said that it has attained the status of a norm at international law which binds all countries, even though the terms of the treaty itself do not yet bind all."[94]

East adduced other elements of state practice in support of a customary prohibition of threat or use of nuclear weapons, including: 1) the non-use of the weapons in war since the bombings of Hiroshima and Nagasaki; 2) regional nuclear weapon free zones such as those established by the Antarctic Treaty, the Treaty of Rarotonga for the South Pacific, and the Treaty of Tlatelolco for Latin America; 3) negative security assurances committing the nuclear weapons states not to use the weapons against non-nuclear weapons states parties to the NPT; 4) the Partial Test Ban Treaty of 1963, which prohibits testing in the atmosphere, under water, or in outer space, and which prohibits underground tests if the explosion would cause the spread of radioactive debris beyond the testing state's jurisdiction; 5) the Outer Space Treaty, Moon Treaty, and Sea-Bed Arms Control Treaty prohibiting stationing nuclear weapons in outer space and on the ocean floor; 6) bilateral arms reductions agreements between the United States and Russia; and 7) the conclusion of conventions to eliminate other weapons of mass destruction, namely biological and chemical weapons.[95]

The nuclear weapon states denied the existence of an international consensus on illegality supporting a customary prohibition on the ground that they and their allies have made nuclear weapons central to their security posture. "As the Court has clearly established," argued State Department lawyer Michael Matheson for the United States, "customary international law is created by a general and consistent practice of States, followed out of sense of legal obligation."[96] He continued,

> No evidence of such practice exists with respect to nuclear weapons, and it cannot be implied from the decision of States possessing such weapons to abstain from using them for hu-

manitarian, political, or military reasons, rather than from a belief, that such abstention was required by law.

In fact, the conduct and publicly-stated views of many States reflect that they do not recognize a general legal obligation to refrain from using nuclear weapons. For example, each of the Permanent Members of the Security Council has made an immense commitment of human and material resources to acquire and maintain stocks of nuclear weapons and their delivery systems, and many other States have decided to rely for their security on these nuclear capabilities.[97]

Rebutting the non-weapon states' reference to a practice of non-use, the United States' McNeill effectively equated use and threat of use, stating:

Mr. President, Members of the Court: we too have lived with the specter of nuclear war for generations. Ours is in every sense a defensive strategy; and very frankly we believe the policy of nuclear deterrence has saved many millions of lives from the scourge of war during the past 50 years. In this special sense, nuclear weapons have been "used," defensively, every day for over half a century – to preserve the peace.[98]

Concerning the Non-Proliferation Treaty, the nuclear weapons states stressed that the treaty recognizes their present possession of nuclear weapons while placing no limitations on threat or use. Thus Matheson argued for the United States that the NPT

can hardly be the basis for a prohibition that goes well beyond its terms and is, in fact, inconsistent with them. Far from prohibiting the possession and use of nuclear weapons by all States, the Non-Proliferation Treaty effectively confirms that the five acknowledged nuclear-weapon States are in lawful possession of such weapons, and calls for negotiations on effective measures to end the nuclear arms race and bring about nuclear disarmament at a future date. This, it seems to us, is clear acknowledgment by the international community that nuclear weapons are not currently prohibited by law, but rather are to be dealt with in future political negotiations among the States parties.[99]

Taking a harder line, the United Kingdom's Lyell challenged the idea that possession of nuclear weapons under the NPT is merely "temporary," suggesting that elimination of nuclear arsenals may have to await "general and complete disarmament," *i.e.* comprehensive, global disarmament governing both conventional arms and weapons of mass destruction.[100]

While not arguing the point specifically, France's Perrin de Brichambaut also linked nuclear and conventional disarmament, stating, for example:

> France has accordingly reaffirmed its commitment to implement Article VI of the Non-Proliferation Treaty which, I would remind you, enjoins all parties to the Treaty, of which France is a signatory, to work towards general and complete disarmament and nuclear disarmament.[101]

The United States did not insist upon the linkage, as shown by Matheson's statement above. Nor did Russia, whose representative Khodakov stated generally:

> [W]e do not want anybody to doubt that the Russian Federation stands for arms control, disarmament, cessation of nuclear weapon tests, and in the long run, for the prohibition of weapons of mass destruction, including nuclear weapons. However, all these restrictions should be introduced as soon as objective conditions necessary to form a common consent of the world community are ripe. We have started to move in this direction. I am quite confident that in future the world community will prohibit nuclear weapons.[102]

The nuclear weapons states and their allies similarly argued that other treaties and commitments placing limitations on possession and use of nuclear weapons confirm that a universal prohibition does not exist. For Germany, Hartmut Hillgenberg of the Ministry of Foreign Affairs argued that states

> have never based their nuclear arms control and disarmament endeavors on the notion of an existing international norm which outlaws nuclear weapons altogether. Negotiations have concentrated – with considerable success – on the non-proliferation of nuclear weapons, the limitation and the reduction of nuclear arsenals and the prohibition of tests, as well as the creation of nuclear-free zones. I submit that this clearly shows that, up to the present moment, there is no convention, international custom or general principle of law which would support that nuclear weapons, as part of a defensive strategy, are illegal under any circumstances.[103]

In reply, Costa Rica's Vargas Pizarro argued regarding nuclear weapon free zones:

> Costa Rica and many other parties to the Treaty [of Tlatelolco] have consistently supported the United Nations General Assembly resolutions which state that the use of nuclear weapons is a crime against humanity, a violation of the United Nations Charter, and/or a violation of international law.... There is no contradiction between seeking agreement from the nuclear States not to threaten or use nuclear weapons in a specific region, and believing that the threat or use is prohibited generally. In fact, the achieving of agreements ... is a confirmation of [that] belief ...[104]

Vargas Pizarro also noted that "among the nuclear-weapon States there is no unanimity concerning the acceptability of threat or use of nuclear weapons," citing China's unqualified no first use commitment and its endorsement of the early conclusion of a nuclear weapons abolition convention, as well as India's written arguments for illegality.[105]

Regarding the NPT, non-weapon states denounced any suggestion that the treaty permits possession of nuclear weapons by the nuclear weapon states for the indefinite future. For Iran, Javad Zarif stated that Article VI of the NPT

> reflects the undertaking of the nuclear powers to end vertical proliferation of nuclear weapons and eventually dismantle their nuclear arsenal as well as the commitment of non-nuclear States to end horizontal proliferation. This mutual undertaking was clearly expressed by the then Prime Minister of the United Kingdom, Harold Wilson: "... The countries which do not possess nuclear weapons and which are now undertaking an obligation not to possess them have the right to expect nuclear-weapon States will fulfill their part of the bargain."
>
> The United States representative, Adrian S. Fisher, stated at the 1968 Geneva Conference that Article VI of the Non-Proliferation of Nuclear Weapons Treaty constitutes a "solemn affirmation of the responsibility of nuclear weapon States to strive for effective measures regarding cessation of the nuclear arms race and disarmament. Moreover, the Article does not make negotiation of [these measures] conditional upon their inclusion within the framework of a treaty on general and complete disarmament."[106]

Mexico's Gonzalez Galvez similarly noted that at the 1995 Review and Extension Conference, Mexico "specifically rejected the argument that by the indefinite extension we were accepting a dichotomy between those countries that have nuclear weapons and those who do not."[107] Gonzalez Galvez also noted Mexico's statement at the conference that it attaches "great importance" to the need to meet the NPT nuclear disarmament obligations, and "should these not be fulfilled, we would need to review our continuation as party to the Treaty..."[108] He summarized, "In short, as a country we are not prepared under any circumstances to accept a monopoly in the possession of nuclear weapons..."[109]

New Zealand's East rejected any linkage between nuclear disarmament and comprehensive conventional disarmament, stating that the NPT

> does not provide a basis for nuclear-weapon States to argue that nuclear arms control and nuclear disarmament can be deferred. Article VI does not make that process conditional on a treaty on general and complete disarmament under strict and effective international control. Such an argument ignores the very *raison d'etre* of the Treaty, which is based on a recognition that nuclear weapons are different. The judgment made was that, in view of the uniquely destructive potential of such weapons, and human nature being what it is, the only option for humanity was to rid itself of these weapons entirely.[110]

In a written reply to a question posed by Judge Schwebel, Malaysia and Zimbabwe demonstrated that the practice of states parties subsequent to adoption of the NPT recognized a distinction between nuclear disarmament and general and complete disarmament. Judge Schwebel asked whether under the NPT "nuclear weapons may be retained in the arsenals of the five nuclear Powers until the achievement of general and complete disarmament under effective international control?"[111] Malaysia and Zimbabwe replied that under the terms of Article VI the obligation to eliminate nuclear weapons applies whether or not a treaty on general and complete disarmament has been achieved.[112] This distinction, they showed, was fully recognized in NPT Review Conferences, the 1978 UN Special Session on Disarmament, and in declarations and commitments made in connection with the 1995 decision to extend indefinitely the NPT.[113] Malaysia and Zimbabwe concluded:

> Any suggestion that nuclear disarmament is dependent upon conventional disarmament erodes the line which the conscience of humanity has drawn between conventional weapons and weapons of mass destruction. It treats in derisory fashion the obligation to achieve elimination of nuclear weapons – the worst of the weapons of mass destruction – because it makes fulfillment of that obligation contingent upon a process for which the world is not yet ready, namely comprehensive conventional disarmament. In contrast to conventional weapons, serious proposals, negotiations, and conventions relating to elimination of weapons of mass destruction including nuclear weapons have been on the

international agenda for decades, including the Geneva Gas Protocol of 1925, the Acheson-Lilienthal proposal for an international agency that would control all weapons usable nuclear materials in the late 1940s, and the biological and chemical weapons conventions concluded in recent years. As appealing as it may sound to some peace advocates, or as convenient an excuse for avoiding reduction and elimination of nuclear arms as it may be for others, there exists no necessary link between nuclear disarmament and general and complete disarmament, nor must any be established, for that would totally negate prospects for elimination of nuclear weapons within a reasonable timeframe.[114]

The United Nations Charter

Article 2(4) of the United Nations Charter provides: "All Members shall refrain in their international relations from the threat or use of force against the territorial integrity or political independence of any state, or in any other manner inconsistent with the Purposes of the United Nations." The first sentence of Article 51 of the Charter provides: "Nothing in the present Charter shall impair the inherent right of individual or collective self-defence if an armed attack occurs against a Member of the United Nations, until the Security Council has taken measures necessary to maintain international peace and security." Under Articles 2(4) and 51, a state may engage in war only in collective or individual self-defence, and then only when the Security Council has not exerted control.

Many of the non-nuclear weapon states did not argue the relevance of the Charter rules governing threat or use of force and self-defence, concentrating instead on rules governing the conduct of warfare. Thus Egypt's Abi-Saad prefaced his examination of humanitarian law: "[W]e are not speaking of the use of force in general, and when it is permitted or prohibited.... The question we have is quite different; it can be formulated as follows: Even when a State has the right to resort to force, in self-defence, can it use nuclear weapons?"[115] Other non-weapon states did, however, argue forcefully that the Article 2(4) prohibition of threat or use of force, and the U.N. Charter generally, preclude threat or use of nuclear weapons in any circumstance.

These states were undoubtedly mindful of the need to establish a general prohibition, which as the supreme treaty in the world the Charter could supply if so interpreted. Also pointing towards this argument were the terms of the General Assembly request for an opinion from the Court and the General Assembly resolutions condemning nuclear weapons. In asking whether the "threat or use of nuclear weapons is permitted in any circumstance," the request tracked the language of Article 2(4) prohibiting the threat or use of force. The 1961 Resolution 1653 declared use of nuclear weapons to be "contrary to the spirit, letter and aims of the United Nations and, as such, a direct violation of the Charter of the United Nations," and this finding was repeated in subsequent resolutions.

For the Philippines, Merlin Magallona, dean and professor of international law at the University of the Philippines, argued:

> [W]ithin the coverage of the peremptory norm of international law on the use of force under Article 2, paragraph 4, of the Charter, the threat or use of nuclear weapons constitutes a special category of acts of State which are the object of interdiction by this norm. Owing to their qualitatively peculiar nature as weapons of mass destruction, nuclear weapons in use occupy a position *sui generis* among the categories of acts embraced by the prohibition of Article 2(4).[116]

The Article 2(4) prohibition of nuclear weapons, he further stated, creates an *erga omnes* obligation owed by every state to the international community as a whole.[117] Referring to related Charter obligations, Magallona asked: "How can a nuclear-weapon Member State claim that it is *performing in good faith* its obligations to refrain from the use of force, to settle disputes by peaceful means, and to establish friendly relations while it is engaged in the threat or use of nuclear weapons?"[118] He concluded,

> In light of these considerations, it becomes logical for the United Nations General Assembly to declare, as it has declared, that the use of nuclear weapons would be a violation in Resolution 1653 [and subsequent resolutions]. These resolutions deserve juridical treatment as interpretations of the Charter."[119]

In its written statement, Malaysia argued that the threat of first use, including a declared policy of threatened first use, violates the United Nations Charter because it

> is inherently a threat against the political independence and territorial integrity of another state. This is true not only when the threat is imminent and aimed at exacting specific changes but also, because of the unique nature of the weapons, when it is a longstanding posture not directly linked to specific demands.[120]

For Costa Rica, Vargas Pizarro told the Court :

> [T]he maintenance by several States of the threat of use of nuclear weapons is fundamentally incompatible with a rational global order as envisioned by the United Nations Charter. The nuclear threat is inherently a threat against the sovereignty of other States and is also inherently contrary to the purposes of United Nations, which include maintenance of international peace and security, and cooperation in the promotion of the achievement of human rights.[121]

On behalf of Indonesia, Johannes Berchmans Soedarmanto Kadisman, Ambassador to the Netherlands, contended:

> [N]othing in Article 51 sanctions a standing threat – a threat *in futuro* – by one State against another, named or unnamed. It sanctions only the use of retaliatory force once an armed attack occurs. Its application is limited to the very brief timespan following an attack; it cannot, therefore, sanction the threat or the use of force as a hypothetical matter inherent in the military doctrine of this or that State.[122]

Berchmans observed that the U.N. Charter was adopted six weeks before the bombing of Hiroshima, and continued,

> The concern of the world community with this new, startling development was evidenced by the fact that the first resolution adopted by the United Nations dealt with the subject of atomic energy and called, *inter alia*, "for the elimination from national armaments of atomic weapons and of all other major weapons adaptable to mass destruction ..."[123]

North Korea, a party to the NPT bound not to acquire nuclear weapons but suspected in the early 1990s of having a nuclear weapon program, stated in a written submission that "the threat or use of nuclear weapons in any case is violation of the UN Charter and the existing international laws, and therefore should not be allowed on any account."[124]

Mexico argued in its written submissions that nuclear weapons cannot be used in self defence under Article 51 of the Charter because such use would violate the requirements of necessity and proportionality. Necessity, in Mexico's formulation, authorizes "only such measures as are strictly necessary to put an end to the attack," and proportionality means "that the size of the measures adopted by an injured State should be comparable to the graveness of the internationally illegal act it is facing and to its effects."[125] Mexico stated that "there is no doubt that a reaction using nuclear weapons to an attack perpetrated with conventional weapons violates the principle of proportionality, which by definition is incompatible with mass destruction."[126] A nuclear response to a nuclear attack, Mexico stated, would violate fundamental principles of international law, especially those applicable to armed conflicts.[127] Further, any justification under the Article 51 right of self defence "would be highly questionable" because "the proportionality of a nuclear response would be uncontrollable and would endanger the security of mankind as a whole."[128]

In response to general arguments based on the U.N. Charter, the nuclear weapons states acknowledged that the Charter rules governing when threat or use of force is permissible apply to nuclear weapons as they do to any weapon. But, they added, this establishes nothing regarding whether the use of nuclear weapons in a war of self defence is prohibited. "There is no legal basis," said Lyell for the United Kingdom, "for rewriting the inherent right of self-defence, recognized in Article 51 of the Charter, so as not to apply to nuclear weapons."[129] For France, Perrin de Brichambaut stated:

> [T]he use of nuclear weapons is authorized in the event of the exercise of the inherent right of individual or collective self-defence. Indeed, neither the customary law applicable to self-defence nor Article 51 of the Charter regulates or limits the military *means* by which States may exercise this right.[130]

The nuclear weapons states also insisted that use of nuclear weapons in self-defence could meet the requirement of proportionality. Lyell argued for the United Kingdom:

> To assume that any defensive use of nuclear weapons must be disproportionate, no matter how serious the threat to the safety and the very survival of the State resorting to such use, is wholly unfounded. Moreover, it suggests an overbearing assumption by the critics of nuclear weapons that they can determine in advance that no threat, including a nuclear, chemical or biological threat, is ever worth the use of any nuclear weapon. It cannot be right to say that if an aggressor hits hard enough, his victim loses the right to take the only measures by which he can defend himself and reverse the aggression.[131]

Those non-weapon states accepting that the U.N. Charter, standing alone, cannot be read to bar threat or use of nuclear weapons, emphasized that, as the weapon states acknowledged, self-defence does not exempt a state from humanitarian and other rules regulating the conduct of warfare. Thus the Solomon Islands' Professor Jean Salmon stated that self defence

> has never authorized a State which is in that situation to use chemical or biological weapons or to annihilate the aggressor's civilian population in defence of its own territory. Why should it permit the use of nuclear weapons with their much more devastating effects?[132]

Non-weapon states also pointed to the paradox that if self defence requires a nuclear weapons capability, then every state should want such a capability. As Zimbabwe's Wutawunashe told the Court:

> The United States and the United Kingdom have argued that military necessity might require the use of nuclear weapons. However, if this assertion were valid, which it is not, the majority of countries would require nuclear weapons in case such a necessity arose, and the current nuclear States would not oppose the spread of nuclear weapons in order that other countries could have, as their right, nuclear weapons for self defence. It would not, I would argue, it would not be too much of a good thing. The fact that the overwhelming majority of countries do not have nuclear weapons, and that nuclear States oppose them acquiring them, indicates the inadmissibility of this proposition.[133]

Threat and Deterrence

In addition to the U.N. Charter prohibition of threat of force for aggressive ends or contrary to U.N. purposes, non-nuclear weapon states invoked humanitarian and other provisions of international law in support of the illegality of threat of use of nuclear weapons. In reply, the nuclear weapon states stressed the value of deterrence to international security, provoking an intense, wide-ranging debate.

The Solomon Islands argued in a written submission:

> [A]ny use of nuclear weapons would *prima facie* violate international humanitarian law. The threat of their use must be considered as totally incompatible with the solemn obligation undertaken by States under common Article I of the four Geneva Conventions of 1949 and Article 1(1) of the 1st 1977 Additional Protocol "to respect and ensure respect" of the four Conventions and the Protocol. Given the inevitability of the lethal effects of nuclear weapons, threatening their use must surely also violate the rights of potential victims as set forth in Article 40 of the 1st Additional Protocol, which provides that "It is prohibited to order that there shall be no survivors, to threaten an adversary therewith or to conduct hostilities on that basis."[134]

Indonesia devoted most of its oral argument to the issue of threat. Berchmans quoted international law scholar Ian Brownlie for the proposition that "[i]f the promise is to resort to force in conditions in which no justification for the use of force exists, the threat itself is illegal."[135] Berchmans also stated that "there is no right to threaten to commit a crime or other illegal act. [If] the use of nuclear weapons is illegal in any circumstance, even by way of self-defence or reprisal, the threat to use nuclear weapons must also be illegal in any circumstance..."[136] He additionally cited the Nuremberg Principles and the Genocide Convention. The Nuremberg Principles prohibit "*planning, preparation,* initiation, or waging of a war of aggression or *a war in violation of international treaties, agreements or assurances.*" Planning and preparation for a war involving the use of nuclear weapons, whether or not aggressive, is prohibited, Berchmans contended, because such a war would entail the commission of war crimes and crimes against humanity, and therefore would be "in violation of international treaties [and] agreements."[137] The Convention on the Prevention and Punishment of the Crime of Genocide of 1948 renders punishable not only genocide, but also *conspiracy*, direct and public *incitement*, and *attempt* to commit genocide, as well as *complicity* in its commission.[138]

The general position of the nuclear weapons states was that the weapons may be used in self-defence under Article 51 of the UN Charter, that their use would not necessarily involve violations of humanitarian law, crimes against humanity, or other violations of international law, and that therefore the threat of use in self-defence is permissible. However, the thrust of their response regarding threat was not so much to engage as to the specifics of its meaning and application under international law as to argue that threat of use of nuclear weapons is integral to the policy of deterrence and therefore to international security. The claim was that nuclear weapons are not so much military means to wage war as political instruments to prevent war. "For France," said Perrin de Brichambaut, "a nuclear weapon is a weapon intended to prevent war by depriving it of any possible rationale."[139] But because deterrence depends on the threat and apparent willingness to employ the weapons in war, the argument had to circle back to the legality of use.

Indeed, the nuclear weapons states implied that because deterrence is essential to international security, threat or use of nuclear weapons must therefore be legal. Thus Matheson argued for the United States:

> If these weapons could not lawfully be used in individual or collective self-defence under any circumstances, there would be no credible threat of such use in response to aggression and deterrent policies would be futile and meaningless. In this sense, it is impossible to separate the policy of deterrence from the legality of the use of the means of deterrence. Accordingly, any affirmation of a general prohibition on the use of nuclear weapons would be directly contrary to one of the fundamental premises of the national security policy of each of these many States.[140]

Perrin de Brichambaut stated for France that "[t]he policy of deterrence publicly stated by [the nuclear weapon] States is meaningful only if the threat of the use of such weapons is not considered unlawful in any circumstance."[141]

The overriding value of deterrence, argued the United Kingdom and France, as well as NATO states Germany and Italy, weighs against the Court rendering an opinion on the merits that could undermine deterrence. Perrin de Brichambaut contended:

France's doctrine of deterrence is the keystone of its security. It also constitutes a pre-eminent factor of stability, more particularly for the European continent, through its positive effects for the allies of France and for the entire international community. It has thus contributed, for several decades, to maintaining that essential asset, world security and peace....

In France's view, the contribution that the policy of deterrence makes to the maintenance of world peace is undeniable, something inseparable from the action taken in regard to disarmament. The mere fact that this is so clearly justifies the store which France sets by this policy. What is more, though – and this is a point I wish to make in all seriousness – I should like to warn against any pronouncement which, directly or indirectly, might imply judgment being passed on a defence policy based on deterrence.[142]

The United Kingdom's Lyell stated:

Since the Second World War, the concept of deterrence has been fundamental to the maintenance of the peace and security of a substantial number of States. Not only the nuclear Powers themselves, but many non-nuclear States have sheltered under the umbrella of these weapons. We might wish nuclear weapons away, as we might wish away all weapons and, indeed, the whole concept of war and coercion. But nuclear weapons do exist and the Court – as a court of law – must operate not in some idealized world but in the real world.... Some start has been made in the reduction of those massive nuclear arsenals which are rightly feared. But huge numbers of nuclear weapons still exist. Our real world remains a fragmented and dangerous place and in this real world, to call in question now the legal basis of the system of deterrence on which so many States have relied for so long for the protection of their peoples could have a profoundly destabilizing effect.[143]

Hillgenberg told the Court for Germany:

[I]n the course of 40 years of Cold War and military stand-off between East and West, Germany has been exposed to the risk of nuclear war in a unique manner. While the Iron Curtain divided Berlin, large nuclear arsenals were accumulated in Europe. Thousands of nuclear weapons were deployed in European countries on both sides of the dividing line in particular on German territory. Germany had to live with the risk of nuclear confrontation on its own soil.

Nevertheless, NATO's strategy of nuclear deterrence as adapted over time has proved successful in preserving peace and freedom. The confrontation of the Cold War years has made room for cooperation and partnership, while the number of nuclear warheads, not only in Europe, has been drastically reduced.

This unique experience, which Germany shared with its friends and allies, must be seen against the background of Germany's total and unambiguous renunciation of nuclear weapons (as well as of other weapons of mass destruction). This was confirmed most recently in the Treaty on the Final Settlement with respect to Germany of 12 September 1990.

Germany has never had and will never possess nuclear weapons. Germany has also continuously advocated an ambitious policy of nuclear arms control and disarmament as a means of enhancing security and stability in Europe and the world....

[T]he fundamental purpose of the Allied nuclear forces is political: to preserve peace and to prevent coercion and any kind of war. The circumstances in which any use of nuclear weapons might have to be contemplated by them are even more remote. Germany, having had to face the risk of becoming the major battlefield in Europe as a result of the East-West confrontation, has always been guided by this fundamental principle of the political character of nuclear weapons, the ultimate deterrence against a threat whose consequences would lead to national catastrophe were it to materialize.

If, against this background, the Court were to assess in any abstract legal manner the hypothetical use of nuclear weapons, this would amount to far more than a purely judicial clarification of a legal question. It would, in the final analysis, directly relate to key security policy considerations. Regardless of the conclusion such an advisory opinion would reach on the matter, it would be a pronouncement on a highly political question.[144]

For Italy, Professor Umberto Leanza of the Ministry of Foreign Affairs advised the Court:

[T]he Italian Government would like to draw the Court's attention to the fact that any reply it might give – regardless of how it might be worded – would ultimately have a political significance that ought in fact never to attach to the decisions of the Court... That part of the [General Assembly] question which refers to the threat of the use of nuclear weapons is even more political, Mr.

President and Members of the Court. This indeed gives rise to even more sensitive problems, inherent in national defence strategies and the conduct of international politics, owing to the generally accepted fact that the power of deterrence, which constitutes the warrant for any threat, is a means of avoiding – not of generating – the use of armed force, through the representation of the ensuing risks. This all the more true in the case of nuclear weapons, whose real effectiveness consists paradoxically in the deterrent power of the threat and not in their actual use.[145]

The non-weapon states took differing, even contradictory, approaches to the deterrence rationale. Many refuted it head on, including one threshold state, India. A handful urged the Court to accommodate deterrence. Among those states that unequivocally condemned deterrence were the following.

For the Philippines, Rodolfo Sanchez, Ambassador to the Netherlands, stated:

Much has been said about nuclear weapons and deterrence. We in the Philippines know very well the concept of deterrence. Like many other nations, we were once ourselves in the grip of this policy. For decades we housed foreign military bases, installations which were part of a global nuclear weapons structure created in the name of deterrence. In 1987, aware of the dangers posed by nuclear weapons and mindful of the growing global opposition to these instruments of destruction, the Filipino people enshrined in the Constitution a provision that declares a policy of freedom from nuclear weapons. Today these foreign bases no longer exist in our land. Today we no longer allow vessels that carry weapons of mass destruction to enter Philippine territory. Today the Philippines is working closely with its neighbours in crafting an agreement to establish a nuclear-weapon-free zone in Southeast Asia.[146]

For Malaysia, Tan Sri Razali Ismail, Ambassador to the United Nations, and subsequently President of the General Assembly, argued to the Court:

The question I would like to ask is why is nuclear deterrence only limited to five countries? The ready answer from the nuclear-weapon states is that their nuclear deterrence contributes to world peace and security. Mr. President, Members of the Court, we have here a very clear case, as is also attendant in the Security Council, where a handful of countries arrogate to themselves, the right to assess and the right to determine what is world peace and security, exclusively in the context of their own national imperatives. What is at best an Atlantic concept of the Cold War, a mindset of the strategy of nuclear powers for over four decades, is being imposed on the whole world....

Five countries cannot arrogate to themselves forever the exclusive privilege of having their finger on the nuclear trigger.... In the final analysis this absurdity of possession, use and threat of use is about power and about hanging on tenaciously to power, to the exclusion of others. The Court is being asked by the nuclear-weapon States, in essence, to perpetuate the right of these five countries to that power apparatus, even when the rest of humanity rejects the diabolical potential interest in nuclear weapons. If the laws of humanity and the dictates of the public conscience demand the prohibition of such weapons, the five nuclear-weapon States, however powerful, cannot stand against them.... International law cannot be utilized to support State practices which deviate from fundamental principles and mainstream aspirations. Otherwise we would be legitimizing the principle that might is right and would have to come to the frightening conclusion that international law is on the side of the powerful, as interpreted by the powerful.[147]

In its written statements, India, known to have at least a nuclear weapons capability, nonetheless opposed deterrence and argued for the illegality of both threat *and* possession, stating:

The use of nuclear weapons in response to attack by a conventional weapon would patently violate the principle of proportionality but also a nuclear response to nuclear attack, would violate the principle of discrimination, humanity, environmental security and probably the principle of neutrality as such an attack would not distinguish between combatants and noncombatants causing civilian casualties, ravaging the natural environment and contaminating the territory of neighboring and distant neutral countries. Nuclear deterrence had been considered to be abhorrent to human sentiment since it implies that a state if required to defend its own existence will act with pitiless disregard for the consequences to its own and adversary's people.

Another question which arises in relation to the theory of deterrence is whether the keeping of peace or the prevention of war is to be made dependent on the threat of horrific indiscriminate destruction which justifies the stockpiling of such weapons at an enormous expense, in the hope that they will merely act as a deterrent but will not in fact be used. However those who do not have such weapons would all the time be racing to build them and those who already have nuclear weapons would continue to develop even more destructive weapons to maintain the superiority necessary for deterrence and this would keep humanity in the perpetual fear of total destruction. A better and saner way to secure everlasting peace would be to ensure that [not] only are such weapons never used but also not made. The security of all nations would best be safeguarded by a nuclear weapon free world. If peace is to be the ultimate objective there can be no doubt that disarmament must be given priority and has to take precedence over deterrence....

Since the production and manufacture of nuclear weapons can only be with the objective of their use, it must follow that if the use of such weapons itself is illegal under international law, then their production and manufacture cannot under any circumstances be considered as permitted. Besides, the manufacture and stockpiling of nuclear weapons would constitute a threat of their eventual use.[148]

In a written submission, Nauru stated:

The principal purpose of the United Nations, as stated in the Preamble to the Charter, is "to save succeeding generations from the scourge of war." Clearly this purpose would be frustrated if a country subjected to a nuclear attack were to retaliate in kind, since the likely outcome of such an exchange would be the massive destruction of life in both countries, not to mention their neighbors and, depending on the size of the exchange, the rest of the planet. A second use of nuclear weapons, in other words, would be impermissible as reprisal and ineffective as well as impermissible as self-defence, since defensive military action is subject to the laws of war to the same extent as offensive military action.

It follows that the doctrine of deterrence, which is the current justification for the stockpiling and potential use of nuclear weapons, is devoid of any basis in the universally accepted norms of humanitarian law.... The prohibition of their use is absolute; it is a rule of *jus cogens* analogous to the rule of human rights law that makes torture a *malum in se* and therefore does not allow for the use of torture in response to torture.[149]

For San Marino, a tiny state situated in Italy, Federica Bigi of the Department of Foreign Affairs raised among other issues the distortion of global priorities:

> The Government of the Republic of San Marino does not support the doctrine of nuclear deterrence, according to which the possession of a nuclear weapon is, in itself, a dissuasive measure. On the contrary, we believe that the possession and threat to use nuclear weapons by a State are a challenge to other States which inevitably results in a further spread of nuclear arsenals.... In a world where millions and millions of human beings are still suffering from underdevelopment and poverty, and dying of hunger and diseases which could not be treated, is it not immoral to invest enormous financial resources in nuclear arsenals? Is not this behavior in conflict with the international commitments undertaken by the States for the promotion of an equitable social development?[150]

For Indonesia, Berchmans told the Court:

> [T]he concept of deterrence insisted upon by the nuclear weapons States as central to their security postures depends on the character of nuclear weapons as weapons of mass destruction whose use could devastate humanity and the earth. Those States cannot now be heard to deny that [the] weapons are weapons of mass destruction whose use is indiscriminate and uncontrollable and therefore illegal. The argument that the threat of use of nuclear weapons has prevented nuclear war is unprovable and speculative in the extreme. Precisely the contrary argument could be made, albeit also in a speculative mode; namely, that deterrence has several times brought the world to the brink of nuclear war and will continue to do so.[151]

Colombia, then serving as head of the Non-Aligned Movement, in a written statement called on the Court to challenge the invocation of the deterrence rationale in relation to "emerging" nuclear weapon states:

> [T]he nuclear dilemma that the world has to confront today must focus attention on the basic illegitimacy of nuclear weapons. [W]ith the end of the Cold War, if not all problems can be solved, at least those that were at the core of the issue such as nuclear deterrence have reached a point of maturity in which the International Court of Justice can declare that the use of nuclear weapons cannot be considered a legitimate mean of self defence

> – if it ever was – and that a commitment must be made by all nuclear powers to the total destruction of these weapons....
>
> An advisory opinion from the International Court of Justice on this issue would most likely interpret the law as applied to every nation, without discriminating between the "national security" and "deterrence" exemption to the law claimed by the nuclear weapon States to justify their own manufacture, development and deployment of such weapons.
>
> Such an advisory opinion would also answer the argument being raised now, that down-scaled nuclear weapons arsenals must be produced and kept in order to cope with emerging small nuclear forces in unstable and aggressive countries. This rationale which pretends to legitimate the use of nuclear weapons, even of their down-scaled version, is a dangerous path that should not be taken or permitted by the international community.[152]

The states most strongly arguing for accommodation of deterrence were the Solomon Islands and Australia. The Solomon Islands' Crawford suggested that because the issue of possession of nuclear weapons is not before the Court by the terms of the General Assembly and WHO requests for advisory opinions, the Court need not address deterrence. Consistent with that state's written submissions, Crawford argued that a specific threat of use of nuclear weapons is prohibited. But, he added, merely maintaining the capability, and hence implicitly deterring potential enemies, is permissible. Crawford told the Court:

> [T]he questions asked in no way cast doubt on the legality of a policy of nuclear deterrence... Deterrence of the kind described by Mr. Perrin de Brichambaut in no way involved a threat of the use of nuclear weapons... There is no present threat to use those weapons, as distinct from the capacity to do so, capacity which is inherent in the distinct concepts of possession and deployment. An armed camp is different from an invasion force, for that matter it is different from a defensive force intending to break the taboo and unleash weapons of mass destruction on the cities of its adversary.
>
> Whether the peace of Europe has been kept by the policy of deterrence is another question. Students of international incidents are as inclined to attribute the non-use of nuclear weapons during the last 45 years to good luck as much as to grand strategy. A still further question is the impact of the nuclear arms race and the policy of deterrence outside Europe.

> But for present purposes the point is simply this: that deterrence and the actual threat to use weapons to achieve one's ends are different things. In this regard Solomon Islands agrees with the definition of "threat" given by France: "a coercive element intended to lead a State to conduct or acts different from those it would otherwise freely choose"... By deterrence a State does not impose any conduct on others which they might otherwise freely choose.
>
> Mr. President, if I may give an illustration: I may be big enough and strong enough to hurt you, if you punch me in the nose, and you may know this, but I am not threatening you, not in the event that you do not punch me in the nose – it is simply a fact. I would add, Mr. President, that I do not know of any aggressor who would not be deterred merely because the possible response might be unlawful. The law does not often enter into the calculations of aggressors.[153]

Australia, which had made far-reaching arguments for the illegality of *possession* as well as threat or use of nuclear weapons, nonetheless also argued in favor of a regime of "stable deterrence." More limited than the Solomon Islands approach, which apparently countenanced implicit deterrence of conventional aggression, Australia argued for deterrence aimed solely at preventing the use of nuclear weapons, pending elimination of nuclear arsenals. Evans told the Court:

> [A]ll States are under an obligation to take positive action to eliminate completely nuclear weapons from the world.... International law must nonetheless deal with the reality of the present existence of large stocks of nuclear weapons. It is accordingly necessary and proper that during the course of the elimination process the principle of stable deterrence be maintained: this would enable for that period the possession or threat of use of nuclear weapons for the sole purpose of ensuring that nuclear weapons are never used by others. Given the inherently illegal nature of nuclear weapons, such deterrence can only be a temporary necessity, and can never make lawful the indefinite possession of threat of use of nuclear weapons.
>
> ... The defence policies of the nuclear-weapon States are based on the principle of stable deterrence. That is, the simultaneous possession of nuclear weapons by the nuclear-weapon States, and the mutually assured destruction which would result from any use of such weapons, deters their use at all. In these circumstances, one nuclear-weapon State cannot be expected unilaterally to undertake a complete nuclear disarmament. This

would undermine the basis of the policy of deterrence, and if anything would make the actual use of nuclear weapons more, rather than less likely. We cannot foresee the future, and should never assume the projection into the indefinite future of present conditions. If the prospect of any nuclear-weapon State initiating a nuclear attack on a nuclear disarmed State looks far-fetched now, it might not be so at some time in the future.

Consistently with this conclusion, Australia, together with many other governments, supports the principle of stable nuclear deterrence pending complete nuclear disarmament. However, we state again that stable deterrence can only be accepted as an interim or transitional condition, that is to say, until the complete elimination of nuclear weapons accompanied by substantial verification provisions is achieved.[154]

The positions of the Solomon Islands and Australia regarding deterrence did not go unchallenged by other non-weapon states. Judge Schwebel asked whether the Solomon Islands' position implies that until nuclear weapons are eliminated, "a nuclear power may continue lawfully to possess nuclear weapons as an implicit deterrent to aggression against it?"[155] Malaysia and Zimbabwe in their written reply rejected any notion that the weapons states can simply maintain their present policies so long as they do not make a specific threat of use of nuclear weapons, emphasizing instead that possession of nuclear weapons may only be temporary and must be mitigated by concrete measures to make possession as non-threatening in possible:

> As long as some states possess nuclear weapons, it is to be expected that other states, at least those not party to any treaty specifically prohibiting such possession, will continue to possess nuclear weapons, whether lawfully or not.
>
> The temporary persistence of a practice declared unlawful, until compliance with a pronouncement of illegality has been achieved, is not without precedent. Depending upon the practice to be eliminated, this may involve a timespan of several years, during which the practice may continue in a state of limbo between legality and illegality, so long as good faith efforts to eliminate it as rapidly as possible are underway....
>
> The temporary persistence of nuclear weapons during a period of transition to abolition could for instance objectively act as an implicit, non-illegal deterrent, if unaccompanied by explicit threats or by the intent to use. Explicit threats, or intent to use, on the other hand, would render possession, even if only temporary, illegal.

What is clear is that all possessing states, in such an event, will continue to be under an obligation to abolish their nuclear weapons as rapidly as possible under a regime of strict and effective international control. (This in no way means that nuclear disarmament is to await general and complete disarmament.) One may add that, whether the deterrent resulting from such temporary possession be implicit or explicit, the illegality of the threat of use of nuclear weapons requires, at the very least, that steps be taken to reduce the threat to the bare minimum. Illustrative implementing measures would include detargeting, dropping launch-on-warning policies, withdrawing nuclear-armed submarines from patrol, separating warheads from delivery systems and disabling the warheads. These temporarily deactivating measures – which can be reactivated in a relatively short period of time – can and should be taken independently of and preliminarily to disarmament steps that physically and permanently eliminate nuclear weapons.[156]

Costa Rica's comments included criticism of the concept of stable deterrence pending abolition advocated by Australia. Vargas Pizarro told the Court:

We consider that it is as difficult to establish that deterrence has kept the peace – or, for that matter, has not kept the peace – as it is to prove that ghosts exist, or do not exist. While the major nuclear Powers have not warred with each other, conventional wars involving those Powers directly or indirectly have raged through out the world. Nor can there be any guarantee that nuclear war will not occur in the future.

The notion of "stable deterrence" is, simply, a myth. For example, former US Secretary of Defense Robert McNamara, in his book *In Retrospect*, has recently written that the Cuban missile crisis of 1962 demonstrates that, so long as the "Great Powers possess large inventories of nuclear weapons, we will face the risk of their use." The argument that nuclear deterrence provides stability is based on the assumption that governments act rationally, that no government would rationally make a decision that could trigger nuclear retaliation, and that nuclear war is unlikely to occur unless deliberately chosen. We consider that all those assumptions are erroneous.

In addition, it should be noted that the value of deterrence, whatever one's view of it, is irrelevant to the questions before the Court. If the threat and use of nuclear weapons are illegal *per se*, they cannot be legitimated by any theory of deterrence. Even were such legitimation possible, it could only be based on a scenario that would totally and unconditionally guarantee the non-use of nuclear weapons forever and a day. Such a scenario cannot seriously be defended in the world in which we live.[157]

Zimbabwe reflected the views of many non-weapon states in holding that the threat of mass destruction inherent in the doctrine of deterrence is no more above the law than other widely condemned practices. Wutawunashe told the Court:

> [I]t seems to us a curious distortion of logic first to create ... a new more dangerous level of armaments ... and [then] seek to persuade others that for the last 50 or so years this new and more dangerous and potentially genocidal level of armaments should be credited with keeping the peace. [W]hile it is true that a minority of states have relied on nuclear deterrence as part of their security doctrine, that does not prove its necessity or legality. The minority of States which engage in torture, arbitrary detention and other forms of gross human rights violations are in the habit of justifying these practices as necessary for their national security, a proposition that has never been accepted by the vast majority of human-rights-respecting states.[158]

Endnotes to Appendix A

Note: Many of the oral and written statements include footnotes, which are not reproduced here.

1. Written Statement of the Government of Ireland re WHO question, p. 3.
2. Written Statement of the Government of Norway re WHO question.
3. Verbatim Record, 9 November 1995, pp. 29-31 (numbering of the paragraphs and emphasis added). The sources referred to in paragraph 2 are Christopher Weeramantry, *Nuclear Weapons and Scientific Responsibility* (1987), p. 84, citing Nagendra Singh, *Human Rights and the Future of Mankind* (1981), p. 93. Weeramantry is presently a judge on the Court, and Singh was formerly a judge and President of the Court.
4. Verbatim Record, 6 November 1995, pp. 48-49.
5. *Effects of Nuclear War on Health and Health Services* (Geneva: WHO, 1984, 2nd ed. 1987).
6. Annex to Verbatim Record, 14 November 1995.
7. Verbatim Record, 6 November 1995, p. 40. The quoted excerpt from the WHO study is from page 7 of the 1987 second edition.
8. Verbatim Record, 7 November 1995, p. 18.
9. *Ibid.*, p. 23.
10. *Ibid.*, pp. 24-26, 28, 32, 35.
11. *Ibid.*, p. 41.
12. *Ibid*, p. 45.
13. Verbatim Record, 14 November 1995, pp. 26-27, 30-31.
14. Verbatim Record, 15 November 1995, pp. 89-90.
15. Verbatim Record, 1 November 1995, p. 39.
16. Written Statement of the Government of Sweden re General Assembly question, p. 3.
17. Verbatim Record, 10 November 1995, p. 52.
18. Verbatim Record, 15 November 1995, p. 85.

[19] *Ibid.*

[20] *Ibid.*, p. 47.

[21] *Ibid.*, pp. 47-49.

[22] *Ibid.*, pp. 87-88.

[23] Verbatim Record, 10 November 1995, pp. 53-54.

[24] *Ibid.*, p. 54.

[25] Verbatim Record, 14 November 1995, p. 30.

[26] Verbatim Record, 15 November 1995 (3 p.m.), pp. 34-35.

[27] Verbatim Record, 14 November 1995, pp. 23, 25.

[28] Article 38 also includes "judicial decisions and the teachings of the most highly qualified publicists [*i.e.*, scholars] of the various nations, as subsidiary means for the determination of rules of law".

[29] Verbatim Record, 30 October 1995, pp. 44-45, 49.

[30] Verbatim Record, 15 November 1995 (3 p.m.), p. 37.

[31] Verbatim Record, 3 November 1995, p. 69.

[32] Verbatim Record, 6 November 1995, p. 45.

[33] Verbatim Record, 14 November 1995, pp. 24-25.

[34] Verbatim Record, 7 November 1995, p. 72.

[35] Verbatim Record, 13 November 1995, p. 56.

[36] *Ibid.*, p. 64.

[37] Verbatim Record, 15 November 1995, p. 98.

[38] *Ibid.*, p. 55.

[39] *Ibid.*

[40] Verbatim Record, 14 November 1995, p. 84.

[41] Verbatim Record, 6 November 1995, p. 41. The prohibition of destruction of property is set forth in Article 23(g) of the Hague Rules on Land Warfare.

[42] International Committee of the Red Cross, *Commentary on the Additional Protocols of 8 June 1977* (1987), p. xxxii, cited in Written Statement of United States re General Assembly question, p. 26.

[43] Verbatim Record, 15 November 1995, p. 42. The United States' position was the same as that of the United Kingdom (*ibid.*, pp. 93-94), as was Russia's, though Russia made no specific reference to provisions regarding reprisals or severe damage to the environment. Verbatim Record, 10 November 1995, p. 52. France, in contrast, denied that Protocol I can be regarded as an authoritative statement of pre-existing law, stating that "although certain provisions of this Protocol are derived from rules and principles of customary international law, they cannot be considered to have supplanted those principles." Verbatim Record (trans.), 2

November 1995, p. 10.

[44] Verbatim Record, 1 November 1995, p. 42.

[45] *Ibid.*, p. 37.

[46] Verbatim Record, 6 November 1995, p. 43.

[47] Verbatim Record, 14 November 1995, p. 72.

[48] Verbatim Record, 6 November 1995, p. 43 (Iran); Verbatim Record, 14 November 1995, p. 74 (Solomon Islands).

[49] Letter dated 16 May 1994 from the Minister for Foreign Affairs of Ukraine re WHO question.

[50] Verbatim Record (trans.), 2 November 1995, p. 9.

[51] Verbatim Record, 15 November 1995, p. 50.

[52] *Ibid.*, p. 51.

[53] Verbatim Record, 14 November 1995, p. 66.

[54] Written Statement of the United States re General Assembly question, p. 30.

[55] Verbatim Record, 15 November 1995, p. 95.

[56] Written Statement of the Netherlands re General Assembly question, p. 12.

[57] Verbatim Record, 3 November 1995, p. 64.

[58] Memorial of the Government of Nauru re WHO question, Part I, p. 26.

[59] Verbatim Record (trans.), 14 November 1995, p. 45.

[60] Written Observations of the Solomon Islands re General Assembly question, para. 3.88, p. 68.

[61] Paras. 79, 83.

[62] Verbatim Record, 1 November 1995, pp. 37, 40.

[63] Verbatim Record, 14 November 1995, p. 84.

[64] Verbatim Record, 6 November 1995, p. 38.

[65] Written Statement of the United States re General Assembly question, pp. 31-32.

[66] Written Comments of the Solomon Islands re WHO question, para. 4.50, pp. 50-51.

[67] Verbatim Record, 15 November 1995, p. 49; Written Statement of the United States re General Assembly question, p. 32.

[68] Verbatim Record, 14 November 1995, p. 67.

[69] Written Statement of Solomon Islands re WHO question, paras. 4.1 – 4.46, pp. 76-95.

[70] Verbatim Record, 14 November 1995, p. 31.

[71] *E.g.*, Verbatim Record, 3 November 1995, p. 36 (Indonesia); Verbatim Record, 7

November 1995, p. 66 (Malaysia); Verbatim Record, 14 November 1995, p. 69 (Solomon Islands).

[72] United Nations, *Report of the Human Rights Committee*, Official Records of the General Assembly, 40th Session, Supplement No. 40 (A/40/40) (1985).

[73] Verbatim Record, 10 November 1995, p. 51.

[74] Verbatim Record (trans.), 2 November 1995, p. 6.

[75] Verbatim Record, 15 November 1995, p. 52.

[76] Verbatim Record, 14 November 1995, p. 70.

[77] *Ibid.*

[78] Verbatim Record, 10 November 1995, p. 43.

[79] *Ibid* at p. 44.

[80] *Ibid* at p. 43.

[81] Verbatim Record, 15 November 1995, pp. 43-44.

[82] Verbatim Record (trans.), 14 November 1995, p. 43.

[83] *Ibid.*, p. 44.

[84] Written Comments of the Solomon Islands re WHO question, paras. 4.47-4.48, pp. 49-50.

[85] Verbatim Record, 15 November 1995, pp. 96-97.

[86] Verbatim Record, 7 November 1995, p. 71

[87] Verbatim Record, 3 November 1995, pp. 65-66.

[88] Verbatim Record, 15 November 1995, p. 62.

[89] Verbatim Record (trans.), 2 November 1995, p. 4.

[90] *Ibid.*, pp. 4-5.

[91] Verbatim Record, 13 November 1995, pp. 58-59.

[92] Verbatim Record, 14 November 1995, pp. 25-26.

[93] Verbatim Record, 30 October 1995, pp. 61-66.

[94] Verbatim Record, 9 November 1995, p. 34-35.

[95] *Ibid.*, pp. 38-50.

[96] Verbatim Record, 15 November 1995, p. 77-78.

[97] *Ibid.*, pp. 77-78.

[98] *Ibid.*, pp. 86-87.

[99] *Ibid.*, pp. 76-77.

[100] Verbatim Record, 15 November 1995, p. 58.

[101] Verbatim Record (trans.), 1 November 1995, p. 34.

[102] Verbatim Record, 10 November 1995, p. 59.

[103] Verbatim Record, 2 November 1995, p. 36.

[104] Verbatim Record, 14 November 1995, pp. 28-29.

[105] *Ibid.*, p. 26-27.

[106] Verbatim Record, 6 November 1995, p. 29. Iran's quotation of Fisher is corrected to substitute "these measures" for "this measure".

[107] Verbatim Record, 3 November 1995, p. 67.

[108] *Ibid.*, p. 68.

[109] *Ibid.*

[110] Verbatim Record, 9 November 1995, p. 36.

[111] Verbatim Record, 3 November 1995, p. 71.

[112] Written Reply of Malaysia and Zimbabwe (jointly submitted) to Questions put by Members of the Court.

[113] *Ibid.* at pp. 2-3.

[114] *Ibid* at pp. 3-4.

[115] Verbatim Record, 1 November 1995, p. 35.

[116] Verbatim Record, 9 November 1995, p. 76.

[117] *Ibid,* p. 78.

[118] *Ibid,* p. 80.

[119] *Ibid.*, p. 81.

[120] Written Statement of Malaysia re General Assembly question, p. 17.

[121] Verbatim Record, 14 November 1995, pp. 31-32.

[122] Verbatim Record, 3 November 1995, pp. 19-20.

[123] *Ibid.*, pp. 31-32.

[124] Letter dated 18 May 1995 from the Permanent Representative of the Democratic People's Republic of Korea re General Assembly question.

[125] Written Statement of Mexico re General Assembly question, p. 10.

[126] *Ibid.*

[127] *Ibid.*

[128] *Ibid.*, p. 11.

[129] Verbatim Record, 15 November 1995, p. 65.

[130] Verbatim Record (trans.), 1 November 1995, p. 68.

[131] Verbatim Record, 15 November 1995, p. 39.

[132] Verbatim Record (trans.), 14 November 1995, p. 33.

[133] Verbatim Record, 15 November 1995 (3 p.m.), p. 33.

[134] Written Observations of the Solomon Islands re General Assembly question, para. 3.10, pp. 25-26.

[135] Verbatim Record, 3 November 1995, p. 27. See Brownlie, *International Law and the Use of Force by States* (1963), p. 364.

[136] Verbatim Record, 3 November 1995, pp. 39-40.

[137] *Ibid.*, pp. 26-27.

[138] *Ibid.*, p. 45.

[139] Verbatim Record (trans.), 1 November 1995, p. 33.

[140] Verbatim Record, 15 November 1995, p. 78.

[141] Verbatim Record (trans.), 2 November 1995, p. 11.

[142] Verbatim Record (trans.), 1 November 1995, pp. 33, 36.

[143] Verbatim Record, 15 November 1995, pp. 22-23.

[144] Verbatim Record, 2 November 1995, pp. 34-35, 38-39.

[145] Verbatim Record (trans.), 6 November 1995, p. 46.

[146] Verbatim Record, 9 November 1995, pp. 63-64.

[147] Verbatim Record, 7 November 1995, pp. 53-54, 56.

[148] Written Statement of India re General Assembly question, pp. 5-6.

[149] Memorial of the Government of Nauru re WHO question, Part I, pp. 28-29.

[150] Verbatim Record, 13 November 1995, pp. 22-23.

[151] Verbatim Record, 3 November 1995, pp. 22-23.

[152] Written Statement of Colombia re WHO question, pp. 1-2.

[153] Verbatim Record, 14 November 1995, pp. 77-78.

[154] Verbatim Record, 30 October 1995, pp. 63-65.

[155] Verbatim Record, 14 November 1995, p. 87. Schwebel's question was: "[I]f as appears from its argument this morning, it is the position of Solomon Islands that the possession of nuclear weapons is not unlawful, whereas the threat or use of nuclear weapons is unlawful, does it follow that, until the achievement of general and complete disarmament under effective control, a nuclear Power may continue lawfully to possess nuclear weapons as an implicit deterrent to aggression against it?"

[156] Written Reply of Malaysia and Zimbabwe to Questions put by Members of the Court (Schwebel's first question of 14 November 1995).

[157] Verbatim Record, 14 November 1995, p. 27.

[158] Verbatim Record, 15 November 1995 (3 p.m.), p. 36.

Appendix B
States' Responses to the Opinion

Non-nuclear weapon states

On 6 November 1996, Malaysia introduced a General Assembly resolution calling for compliance with the ICJ opinion. The resolution eventually had more than 40 co-sponsors and was adopted on 10 December 1996 with the support of 115 states. The nuclear weapon states, other than China, were opposed. In a separate vote, a paragraph underlining the Court's statement of the obligation to eliminate nuclear weapons was supported by 139 states, including such Western-aligned states as Australia, Japan, and Canada. The principal thrust of the resolution was to call for the commencement in 1997 of negotiations leading towards a nuclear weapons convention. (For the full text, see Appendix E.) Despite the overwhelming support for this recommendation, such negotiations cannot begin in the Conference on Disarmament in Geneva without the consent of the nuclear weapon states.

In introducing the resolution, Malaysian Ambassador Hasmy Bin Agam stated that the opinion "by the highest international legal authority is of historic importance and cannot be dismissed." He continued:

> It is important in that it has set the legal parameters whereby the use of nuclear weapons indeed ignores customary international law and international treaties such as the Geneva and Hague Conventions. It is important, also, for the reason that it points the direction of international action in addressing this issue upon which hinges the very survival of mankind. The threat to its survival by the existence of nuclear weapons grants the international community the right to take a position on the legality of such weapons.
>
> [Co-sponsors of the resolution] share Malaysia's conviction that the Court's opinion is an important and positive development in the nuclear disarmament process, and should be built on. It would not be enough to merely take note of it, or even to welcome it, and then to forget about it. The learned judges of the ICJ have made it very clear that the international community has not only an obligation to pursue "negotiations leading to nuclear

disarmament in all its aspects," (*i.e.*, in accordance with Article VI of the Nuclear Non-Proliferation Treaty), but also to "bring to a conclusion" such negotiations.... The Court has unanimously affirmed that the obligation to negotiate on nuclear disarmament in all its aspects belongs to *all* States, both nuclear and non-nuclear ... It is clear that the obligation to negotiate on nuclear disarmament exists independently and is not linked to negotiations on a treaty on general and complete disarmament.

[M]y delegation commends [the resolution] for the consideration, co-sponsorship or support of all delegations who share these sentiments and are opposed to the threat or use of nuclear weapons and who would like to ensure that concrete and effective steps are taken now to pave the way for their total elimination within a realistic time-frame, in the interest of ensuring the well-being and survival of humanity.[1]

As the broad support for the resolution indicates, the reaction of non-nuclear weapon states to the opinion was generally positive. For example, on 9 July 1996, President Fidel Ramos of the Philippines stated:

I welcome the decision of the International Court of Justice (ICJ) ... declaring that a threat or use of force by means of nuclear weapons would be contrary to the rules of international law applicable in armed conflict.

The Philippines has vehemently campaigned against the use or threat or force of nuclear weapons on a number of occasions, which culminated in its submission of oral arguments in November 1995 before the ICJ... This landmark decision, therefore, gives justice to the arduous task that the Philippines has launched to achieve a nuclear weapons free world.

Given this development in international law, and consistent with the Philippine constitutional position against nuclear weapons, I would like to sound, once more, our call for the immediate convening of the states parties to the Nuclear Non-Proliferation Treaty to negotiate a comprehensive Nuclear Weapons Convention pursuant to their obligation and responsibility under Article VI of the said treaty.

---

[1] Statement by H.E. Ambassador Hasmy Bin Agam, Alternative Permanent Representative of Malaysia to the United Nations, in Introducing the Draft Resolution A/C.1/51/L.37 on Advisory Opinion of the International Court of Justice on the Legality of the Threat or Use of Nuclear Weapons, at the First Committee of the 51st Session of the United Nations General Assembly, 6 November 1996.

Germany, another non-nuclear weapon state, but one that is part of nuclear-armed NATO, in a 25 August 1997 letter responded to a challenge to NATO's reliance on nuclear weapons as follows:

> The ICJ made it clear that the Article VI of the NPT does not end with a procedural duty to negotiate; rather the duty is to accomplish a certain goal - nuclear disarmament in all its aspects. The German government agrees with this legal interpretation.
>
> In its advisory opinion, the ICJ left completely open whether the use of nuclear weapons in an extreme case of self-defence, in which the survival of a state would be at stake, would be lawful. The ICJ consequently did not state that possession of nuclear weapons by the nuclear weapon states and nuclear deterrence are contrary to international law.[2]

Nuclear weapon states

In a press statement on the day the opinion was issued, 8 July 1996, the United States Department of State commented:

> The Court found there is no comprehensive and universal prohibition on the threat or use of nuclear weapons. The Court declined to pass on the policy of nuclear deterrence. Its opinion indicates that the use of nuclear weapons in some circumstances would be legal. The position of the United States supporting the legality of use of nuclear weapons is as we told the Court. We believe that the use of such weapons would be legal when they are used in compliance with the law of armed conflict applicable to all weapons.
>
> Nuclear deterrence has played a vital role in maintaining our common security and defending the United States and its allies over the past 50 years. Nuclear deterrence continues to make an essential contribution to preserving peace, security, and stability. We do not believe that the Court's opinions provide reason to alter the common defense policy of the United States and its allies.
>
> These are advisory opinions of the Court. Advisory opinions state the Court's views on legal questions asked by international organizations. They are not binding on governments.

The Russian Foreign Ministry made the following statement:

---

[2] Letter dated 25 August 1997 from Dr. Scharioth, German Foreign Office, Bonn, to Pol D'Huyvetter (unofficial translation).

Having ruled that the threat or use of nuclear weapons would generally be contrary to the international law of armed conflicts, the Court has admitted that it had failed to come to a final conclusion whether the threat or use of nuclear weapons could be legal under extreme circumstances of self-defence when the very existence of state is under question. Such controversial, on the surface, decision of the World Court on nuclear issues has in fact reflected a complex, mostly political role of the nuclear weapons in modern world. That has been recognized in a number of international treaties, official doctrines and government declarations. Nuclear weapons prime task is to provide nuclear containment, that is to prevent war, mainly global conflict. Military aspect of nuclear weapons is nothing but only a background for its key political function. Nuclear weapons in its military nature can be used only as last-resort means under quite extraordinary circumstances.

Nuclear weapon has never actually been used in post-war military conflicts. Today a possibility of its use is substantially less than ever in the past, let alone Cold War period. Positive development of international situation, overcoming of confrontation, strengthening of spirit of partnership and cooperation allow to make stronger emphasis on non-military, *i.e.*, political, legal, economic means to prevent and confront violations of peace.

On the other hand, progress in nuclear disarmament along with consolidation of nuclear non-proliferation regime is gaining momentum. It is not accidental, therefore that World Court has determined that there exists an obligation under international law to pursue in good-faith and bring to a conclusion nuclear disarmament negotiations. Russian side is entirely committed to the goals of nuclear disarmament and non-proliferation and is going to work hard to achieve them.[3]

On the day the opinion was released, a French Foreign Ministry spokesperson stated:

France takes note of the opinion given by the International Court of Justice on the question of the legality of the use or threat of nuclear weapons. These opinions, which are not acts of jurisprudence, have no compulsory force.

---

[3] Statement quoted in 1 November 1996 letter of Sergei Belyaev, Russian Ambassador to New Zealand, to John Hampton.

> [The opinion] recognizes that the use or threat of nuclear weapons may be legal in exceptional circumstances of legitimate self-defence as defined in Article 51 of the United Nations Charter. That is also France's position.
>
> Nuclear deterrence is aimed at prohibiting any threat to our vital interests, as defined in the last resort by the head of state.[4]

For the United Kingdom, Lord Earl Howe, government spokesperson on defence matters, stated in the House of Lords on 12 July 1996:

> The opinion of the Court has no implications at all for our defence policy. We see no reason to change the fundamental elements of UK and NATO defence policy. Like the Court, we believe that the use of nuclear weapons would be considered only in self-defence in extreme circumstances. For the UK, self-defence must include collective defence. I believe that it is right for me to emphasize that ... nuclear forces continue to have an essential role within our defence posture and that of NATO and that we shall retain them as long as they are necessary for our security.

A year later, in a Ministry of Defence letter, the new British government responded to criticism of its nuclear-armed submarine, Trident, as follows:

> The goal of the Government is the global elimination of nuclear weapons. The Government will therefore press for multilateral negotiations towards mutual, balanced and verifiable reductions in nuclear weapons and when satisfied with progress towards this goal, will include British nuclear weapons in these negotiations. The Government has made it clear that, it will retain Trident to provide a minimum, but effective and credible deterrent, while working towards this goal.
>
> The International Court of Justice (ICJ) Advisory Opinion is long and complex. But the Court clearly did not rule nuclear weapons to be illegal. It concluded by a large majority that there is in international law no comprehensive and universal prohibition of the threat of use of nuclear weapons as such. It was unable to offer a definitive opinion on whether the use or threat of use of nuclear weapons would be unlawful in all circumstances. The Government is confident that the Opinion does not require a

---

[4] Reuters news dispatch, 8 July 1996, "France Says World Court Upholds Its Nuclear Stance".

change in the United Kingdom's or NATO's nuclear deterrence policy.[5]

In an 8 August 1996 letter responding to an inquiry concerning the opinion, the Chinese Embassy to New Zealand reiterated China's policy that in no circumstance would it be the first to use nuclear weapons and its commitment to realization of a nuclear weapon free world at an early date.[6]

---

[5] Letter dated 3 July 1997 from Mrs. S. James, UK Ministry of Defense, to Miss M. Elabor.

[6] Letter dated 8 August 1996 from Zhigang Fu to Arthur Quinn.

Appendix C
World Health Assembly Resolution WHA46.40, Adopted 14 May, 1993, Requesting Advisory Opinion

The Forty-sixth World Health Assembly,

Bearing in mind the principles laid down in the WHO Constitution;

Noting the report of the Director-General on health and environmental effects of nuclear weapons[1];

Recalling resolutions WHA34.38, WHA36.28 and WHA40.24 on the effects of nuclear war on health and health services;

Recognizing that it has been established that no health service in the world can alleviate in any significant way a situation resulting from the use of even one single nuclear weapon[2];

Recalling resolutions WHA42.26 on WHO's contribution to the international efforts towards sustainable development and WHA45.31 which draws attention to the effects on health of environmental degradation and recognizing the short- and long-term environmental consequences of the use of nuclear weapons that would affect human health for generations;

Recalling that primary prevention is the only appropriate means to deal with the health and environmental effects of the use of nuclear weapons[2];

Noting the concern of the world health community about the continued threat to health and the environment from nuclear weapons;

Mindful of the role of WHO as defined in its Constitution to act as the directing and coordinating authority on international health work (Article 2 *(a)*); to propose conventions, agreements and regulations (Article 2 *(k)*); to report on administrative and social techniques affecting public health from preventive and curative points of view (Article 2 *(p)*); and to take all necessary action to attain the objectives of the Organization (Article 2 *(v)*);

---

[1] Document A46/30.

[2] See *Effects of Nuclear War on Health and Health Services* (2nd ed.), Geneva, WHO, 1987.

Realizing that primary prevention of the health hazards of nuclear weapons requires clarity about the status in international law of their use, and that over the last 48 years marked differences of opinion have been expressed by Member States about the lawfulness of the use of nuclear weapons;

1. *Decides*, in accordance with Article 96(2) of the Charter of the United Nations, Article 76 of the Constitution of the World Health Organization and Article X of the Agreement between the United Nations and the World Health Organization approved by the General Assembly of the United Nations on 15 November 1947 in its resolution 124 (II), to request the International Court of Justice to give an advisory opinion on the following question:

> In view of the health and environmental effects, would the use of nuclear weapons by a State in war or other armed conflict be a breach of its obligations under international law including the WHO Constitution?

2. *Requests* the Director-General to transmit this resolution to the International Court of Justice, accompanied by all documents likely to throw light upon the question, in accordance with article 65 of the Statute of the Court.

Appendix D
General Assembly Resolution 49/75 K, Adopted 15 December 1994, Requesting Advisory Opinion

The General Assembly,

Conscious that the continuing existence and development of nuclear weapons pose serious risks to humanity,

Mindful that States have an obligation under the Charter of the United Nations to refrain from the threat or use of force against the territorial integrity or political independence of any State.

Recalling its resolutions 1653 (XVI) of 24 November 1961, 33/71 B of 14 December 1978, 34/83 G of 11 December 1979, 35/152 D of 12 December 1980, 36/92 I of 9 December 1981, 45/59 B of 4 December 1990 and 46/37 D of 6 December 1991, in which it declared that the use of nuclear weapons would be a violation of the Charter and a crime against humanity,

Welcoming the progress made on the prohibition and elimination of weapons of mass destruction, including the Convention on the Prohibition of the Development, Production and Stockpiling of Bacteriological (Biological) and Toxin Weapons and on Their Destruction[1] and the Convention on the Prohibition of the Development, Production, Stockpiling and Use of Chemical Weapons and on Their Destruction,[2]

Convinced that the complete elimination of nuclear weapons is the only guarantee against the threat of nuclear war,

Noting the concerns expressed in the Fourth Review Conference of the Parties to the Treaty on the Non-Proliferation of Nuclear Weapons that insufficient progress had been made towards the complete elimination of nuclear weapons at the earliest possible time,

---

[1] Resolution 2826 (XXVI), Annex.

[2] See *Official Records of the 47th Session of the General Assembly, Supplement No. 27* (A/47/27), Appendix I.

Recalling that, convinced of the need to strengthen the rule of law in international relations, it has declared the period 1990-1999 the United Nations Decade of International Law,[3]

Noting that Article 96, paragraph 1, of the Charter empowers the General Assembly to request the International Court of Justice to give an advisory opinion on any legal question,

Recalling the recommendation of the Secretary-General, made in his report entitled 'An Agenda. for Peace,'[4] that United Nations organs that are authorized to take advantage of the advisory competence of the International Court of Justice turn to the Court more frequently for such opinions,

Welcoming resolution 46/40 of 14 May 1993 of the Assembly of the World Health Organization, in which the organization requested the International Court of Justice to give an advisory opinion on whether the use of nuclear weapons by a State in war or other armed conflict would be a breach of its obligations under international law, including the Constitution of the World Health Organization,

Decides, pursuant to Article 96, paragraph 1, of the Charter of the United Nations, to request the International Court of Justice urgently to render its advisory opinion on the following question: 'Is the threat or use of nuclear weapons in any circumstance permitted under international law?'

---

[3] Resolution 44/23.

[4] A/47/277-S/24111.

Appendix E

General Assembly Resolution 51/45 M, Adopted 10 December 1996, Calling for Compliance with Advisory Opinion by Commencement of Negotiations Leading Toward a Nuclear Weapons Convention

The General Assembly,

Recalling its resolution 49/75 K of 15 December 1994, in which it requested the International Court of Justice to render an advisory opinion on whether the threat or use of nuclear weapons is permitted in any circumstance under international law,

Mindful of the solemn obligations of States parties, undertaken in Article VI of the Treaty on the Non-Proliferation of Nuclear Weapons,[1] particularly to pursue negotiations in good faith on effective measures relating to cessation of the nuclear arms race at an early date and to nuclear disarmament,

Recalling its resolution 50/70 P of 12 December 1995, in which it called upon the Conference on Disarmament to establish an ad hoc committee on nuclear disarmament to commence negotiations on a phased programme of nuclear disarmament and for the eventual elimination of nuclear weapons within a time-bound framework,

Recalling also the Principles and Objectives for Nuclear Non-Proliferation and Disarmament adopted at the 1995 Review and Extension Conference of the Parties to the Treaty on the Non-Proliferation of Nuclear Weapons,[2] and in particular the objective of determined pursuit by the nuclear-weapon States of systematic and progressive efforts to reduce nuclear weapons globally with the ultimate goal of eliminating those weapons,

---

[1] United Nations, *Treaty Series*, vol. 729, No. 10485.

[2] See *1995 Review and Extension Conference of the Parties to the Treaty on the Non-Proliferation of Nuclear Weapons, Final Document, Part I* (NPT/CONF.1995/32 (Part I)).

Recognizing that the only defense against a nuclear catastrophe is the total elimination of nuclear weapons and the certainty that they will never be produced again,

Desiring to achieve the objective of a legally binding prohibition of the development, production, testing, deployment, stockpiling, threat or use of nuclear weapons and their destruction under effective international control,

Reaffirming the commitment of the international community to the goal of the total elimination of nuclear weapons, and welcoming every effort towards this end,

Reaffirming the central role of the Conference on Disarmament as the single multilateral disarmament negotiating forum,

Noting the adoption of the Comprehensive Test Ban Treaty by the General Assembly in its resolution 50/245 of 10 September 1996,

Regretting the absence of multilaterally negotiated and legally binding security assurances from the threat or use of nuclear weapons against non-nuclear weapon states,

Convinced that the continuing existence of nuclear weapons poses a threat to all humanity and that their use would have catastrophic consequences for all life on Earth,

1. *Expresses* its appreciation to the International Court of Justice for responding to the request for an advisory opinion made by the General Assembly at its forty-ninth session;

2. *Takes note* of the International Court of Justice Advisory Opinion on the Legality of the Threat or Use of Nuclear Weapons issued on 8 July 1996;[3]

3. *Underlines* the unanimous conclusion of the Court that there exists an obligation to pursue in good faith and bring to a conclusion negotiations leading to nuclear disarmament in all its aspects under strict and effective international control;

4. *Calls upon* all States to fulfill that obligation immediately by commencing multilateral negotiations in 1997 leading to an early conclusion of a nuclear-weapons convention prohibiting the development, production, testing, deployment, stockpiling, transfer, threat or use of nuclear weapons and providing for their elimination;

5. *Requests* the Secretary-General to provide the necessary assistance to support the implementation of this resolution;

6. *Decides* to include in the provisional agenda of its fifty-second session an item entitled "Follow-up to the Advisory Opinion of the International Court of Justice on the Legality of the Threat or Use of Nuclear Weapons."

---

[3] *Legality of the Threat or Use of Nuclear Weapons, Advisory Opinion*, A/51/218, annex; see also *Official Records of the General Assembly, Fifty-first Session, Supplement No. 4* (A/51/4), paras. 176-183.

Further Reading

Where to Find the Opinion

The Court's nuclear weapons advisory opinion (including the judges' separate statements), UN document A/51/218 (15 October 1996), is available in English at cost from:

United Nations Publications
Two United Nations Plaza, DC2-853
New York, New York 10017 USA
Tel: +1 212 963 8302; Fax: +1 212 963 3489
E-mail: publications@un.org

It is also available in many law libraries at 35 International Legal Materials 814 (No. 4, July 1996) (English), and eventually will be published as part of the official ICJ Reports. If you have difficulty obtaining the opinion or other materials listed below, contact IALANA or LCNP (see "Contacts").

The opinion and the judges' separate statements can additionally be found at the IALANA website, http://www.ddh.nl/org/ialana (English or French). The Court's opinion regarding the World Health Assembly request as well as its opinion in reply to the General Assembly can be found at http://www.inter.nl.net/hcc/A.Malten/docs.html.

Articles, books, and papers concerning the opinion and the history of the case that have come to IALANA's attention to date are listed below; the list is not intended to be exhaustive.

Assessment of the Opinion

Agni: Studies in International Strategic Issues (Vol. 2, No. 2, September-December 1996), "International Court of Justice Advisory Opinion," pp. 27-36, "World Court Advisory Opinion Begins to Bite," pp. 37-43

Francis A. Boyle, "The Criminality of Nuclear Deterrence" (College of Law, University of Illinois at Urbana-Champaign, October 17, 1996)

George Bunn, "The Legal Status of U.S. Negative Security Assurances to Non-Nuclear Weapon States," 4 *Nonproliferation Review* (No. 3, Spring-Summer 1997), pp. 1-17

Roger Clark, "The Laws of Armed Conflict and the Use or Threat of Use of Nuclear Weapons," 7 *Criminal Law Forum* (No. 2, 1996), pp. 265-296

Dieter Deiseroth, "Der Internationale Gerichtshof und die Atomwaffenfrage," *Betrifft Justiz* (No. 48, December 1996)

Disarmament Times (Vol. XIX, No. 4, September 1996), special issue, with articles by Kate Dewes and Robert Green, William Epstein, Roger K. Smith, Kenji Urata, and Peter Weiss

Richard Falk, "Nuclear Weapons, International Law and the World Court: An Historic Encounter," 91 *American Journal of International Law* (No. 1, January 1997) pp. 64-75

T.D. Gill, "Naschrift," 86 *Militair Rechtelijk Tijdschrift* (November-December 1996), pp. 407-410

Ann Fagan Ginger, ed., *Nuclear Weapons Are Illegal: The Historic Opinion of the World Court and How It Will Be Enforced*, forthcoming, Apex Press, New York, with an introduction by Ann Fagan Ginger

Robert Green, "Nuclear Weapons: The Legality Issue," 11 *Medicine and War* (No. 3, July-September 1995), special Hiroshima and Nagasaki 50th anniversary issue, pp. 79-88

IALANA, ed., *Atomwaffen vor dem Internationalen Gerichtshof: Dokumentation – Analysen – Hintergrunde* (Muenster: Lit Verlag, 1997)

International Review of the Red Cross (No. 316, January 1997), foreword by Judge Géza Herczegh, articles by Yves Sandoz, Luigi Condorelli, Eric David, Louise Doswald-Beck, Hisakazu Fujita, Christopher Greenwood, Timothy L.H. McCormack, Manfred Mohr, and John H. McNeill; also available at http://www.icrc.org

David Krieger, "Nuremberg and Nuclear Weapons," *Medicine & Global Survival* (23 July 1997), on-line journal at http://www.healthnet.org/MGS

Marie-Pierre Lanfranchi and Theodore Christakis, *La Licéité de l'Emploi d'Armes Nucléaires devant la Cour Internationale de Justice, Analyse et Documents* (Paris: Economica, 1997)

Michael J. Matheson, "The Opinions of the International Court of Justice on the Threat or Use of Nuclear Weapons," 91 *American Journal of International Law* (No. 3, July 1997), pp. 417-435

Saul Mendlovitz and Merav Datan, "Advisory Opinion on the Legality of the Threat or Use of Nuclear Weapons: A Narrative of Affirmative Appreciation and Judge Weeramantry's Grotian Quest," forthcoming in *Legal Visions of the Twenty-First Century: Essays in Honor of Judge Christopher Weeramantry*, Martinus Nijhoff Publishers, Dordrecht

Ryszard Piotrowicz, "The world court judges nuclear weapons unjudgeable," 70 *Australian L. J.* (December 1996), pp. 959-962

Situation, Journal du Centre Recherche Droit International (No. 28, Winter 1996-1997), "Dossier: La Cour Internationale de Justice et les Armes Nucléaires," articles by Jonathan Selvadoray, Danielle Jose, Olivier Russbach, and Frédéric Gouin

Rupert Ticehurst, "The Advisory Opinion of the International Court of Justice on the legality of the threat or use of nuclear weapons," *War Studies Journal* (Autumn 2(1), 1996), pp. 107-118

Rupert Ticehurst, "The Martens Clause and the Laws of Armed Conflict," *International Review of the Red Cross* (No. 317, March-April 1997), pp. 125-134; also available at http://www.icrc.org

Alyn Ware, "Bombs Away? The World Court Decision on Nuclear Weapons," *Disarmament Diplomacy* (No. 8, September 1996), pp. 18-20

Peter Weiss, "And now, abolition," *The Bulletin of the Atomic Scientists* (September/October 1996), pp. 42-43; also articles by Mike Moore, Jeremy J. Stone, Michael Krepon, and Kathleen Bailey

Peter Weiss, "Notes on a Misunderstood Decision: the World Court's Near Perfect Advisory Opinion in the Nuclear Weapons Case," *Medicine & Global Survival* (23 July 1997), on-line journal at http://www.healthnet.org/MGS

The World Court Project, *Implications of the Advisory Opinion by the International Court of Justice on the Legal Status of Nuclear Weapons* (London: The Pottle Press, 1996) (available from World Court Project UK, listed in "Contacts")

Background on the Case and the Hearings

John Burroughs and Jacqueline Cabasso, "Nukes on Trial," *The Bulletin of the Atomic Scientists* (March/April 1996), pp. 41-45.

Roger S. Clark and Madeleine Sann, eds., *The Case against the Bomb: Marshall Islands, Samoa, and Solomon Islands before the International Court of Justice in Advisory Proceedings on the Legality of the Threat or Use of Nuclear Weapons* (Camden, NJ, USA: Rutgers University School of Law, 1996)

Katie Boanas-Dewes, "Participatory Democracy in Peace and Security Decision Making," 5 *Interdisciplinary Peace Research* (No. 2, October-November 1993), pp. 80-108

Kate Dewes and Robert Green, "The World Court Project: How A Citizen Network Can Influence The United Nations," 7 *Pacifica Review* (No. 2, 1995), pp. 17-37

Erich Geiringer, "The World Court Project: Nuclear Weapons on Trial," in *A Prescription for Global Health and Security*, Proceedings of IPPNW's Fourth

Asia-Pacific Regional Conference, August 4-7, 1994, Ron McCoy, ed., 1 June 1996

Robert Green and Kate Dewes, "The World Court Project: How a Citizen Network Can Influence the United Nations," 15 *Social Alternatives* (No. 3, July 1996), pp. 35-37

Nicholas Grief, *The World Court Project on Nuclear Weapons and International Law: A Joint Project of the International Association of Lawyers Against Nuclear Arms, the International Peace Bureau, and the International Physicians for the Prevention of Nuclear War* (Northampton, MA, USA: Aletheia Press, 2d ed. 1993)

Saul Mendlovitz and Peter Weiss, "Judging the Illegality of Nuclear Weapons: Arms Control Moves to the World Court," *Arms Control Today* (February 1996), pp. 10-14

Keith Mothersson, *From Hiroshima to The Hague: A Guide to the World Court Project* (Geneva: International Peace Bureau, 1982)

Mary Riseley and Karin Salzman, "Nuclear Weapons On Trial," *Santa Fe Reporter*, November 29–December 3, 1995, pp. 15-20

Nicholas Rostow, "The World Health Organization, the International Court of Justice, and nuclear weapons," 20 *Yale Journal of International Law* (No. 1, Winter 1995), pp. 151-185

Roger K. Smith, "The Bomb on the Docket: The World Court Scrutinizes Nuclear Weapons," NGO Committee on Disarmament website, http://www.igc.apc.org/disarm/icjpiece.html

Peter Weiss, Burns H. Weston, Richard A. Falk, and Saul H. Mendlovitz, "Draft Memorial in Support of the Application by the World Health Organization for an Advisory Opinion by the International Court of Justice on the Legality of the Use of Nuclear Weapons Under International Law, Including the WHO Constitution," 4 *Transnational Law & Contemporary Problems* (No. 2, Fall 1994), pp. 721 – 823

Case and Other Materials

Model briefs prepared by IALANA/LCNP lawyers; states' written submissions and written replies to judges' questions, and transcripts of states' oral argument before the ICJ; *Banning the Bomb*, a report on the hearings with excerpts of states' arguments; and the Model Nuclear Weapons Convention and supporting documents are available from the Lawyers' Committee on Nuclear Policy (see "Contacts").

Note: IALANA would appreciate information about relevant articles, books, papers and other materials not listed above.

Contacts

International Association of Lawyers
 Against Nuclear Arms
Anna Paulownastraat 103
2518 BC The Hague
Netherlands
Tel: +31 70 363 4484
Fax: +31 70 345 5951
E-mail: ialana@antenna.nl
Website: http://www.ddh.nl/org/ialana

International Physicians for the Prevention
 of Nuclear War
126 Rogers Street
Cambridge, Massachusetts 02142
United States
Tel: +617 868 5050
Fax: +617 868 2560
E-mail: ippnwbos@igc.apc.org
Website:
 http://www.healthnet.org/IPPNW

International Peace Bureau
41 rue de Zurich
1201 Geneva
Switzerland
Tel: +41 22 731 6429
Fax: +41 22 738 9419
E-mail: ipb@gn.apc.org
Website: http://www3.itu.int/ipb

Lawyers' Committee on Nuclear Policy
666 Broadway, Suite 625
New York, New York 10012
United States
Tel: +1 212 674 7790
Fax: +1 212 674 6199
E-mail: lcnp@aol.com

Western States Legal Foundation
1440 Broadway, Suite 500
Oakland, California 94612
United States
Tel: +1 510 839 5877
Fax: +1 510 839 5397
E-mail: wslf@igc.apc.org

Russian IALANA
Alexander Sukharev or
 Korolkov Nickolay
Releyeva St. 4
Moscow, 103885
Russia
Tel: +70 95 2900 337
Fax: +70 95 256 5463

Japanese Association of Lawyers Against
 Nuclear Arms (JALANA)
Masanori Ikeda
Yotsuya Law Office
ITO Building 7F
1-2 Yotsuya, Shinjuku-ku
Tokyo, 160
Japan
Tel: +81 333 41 1417
Fax: +81 333 41 1439

Swedish Lawyers Against Nuclear Arms
Stig Gustafsson
c/o TCO, Box 5252
Stockholm, 10245
Sweden
Tel: +46 87 82 9118
Fax: +46 86 63 7520

IALANA Germany
Peter Becker
Postfach 1168
Marburg, D-35037
Germany
Tel: +49 64 212 3027
Fax: +49 64 211 5828

Norsk Medlemsgruppe
Fredrik S. Heffermehl
IALANA
Niels Juelsgatan 28A
Oslo 2, 9272
Norway
Tel: +47 224 48003
Fax: +47 224 47616

Association of Italian Democratic Lawyers
Fabio Marcelli
c/o CNR
Ciso Vittorio, Emanuele II, 251
Rome, 00186
Italy
Tel: +39 6689 3009
Fax: +39 6683 0 8307

Italian Lawyers Against Nuclear Arms
Joachim Lau
Casa Aiale
Salutio, I-52010
Italy
Tel and fax: +39 575 59 2243

Juristen tegen Kernwapens
Dirk de Bruijn
Frits van den Berghelaan 167
Aartselaar, B 2630
Belgium
Tel: +32 3887 1628
Fax: +32 2640 0774

IALANA UK
Rupert Ticehurst
King's College Faculty of Law
Strand
London, WC2R 2LS
United Kingdom
Tel: + 44 171 83 6 5454 (ext. 1269)
Fax: +44 171 87 3 2465

Lawyers for Social Responsibility
Beverly Delong
5120 Carney Road N.W.
Calgary, Alta, T2L 1G2
Canada
Tel: +1 403 282 8260
Fax: +1 403 289 4272

World Court Project UK
87 Summerheath Road
Hailsham, Sussex BN27 3DR
United Kingdom
Tel and fax: +44 1323 844 269
E-mail: geowcpuk@gn.apc.org

World Court Project Aotearoa
Post Office Box 8390
Riccarton, Christchurch
New Zealand
Tel and fax: +64 3 348 1353
E-mail: katie@chch.planet.org.nz

World Court Project Canada
Physicians for Global Survival
145 Spruce Street, Suite 208
Ottawa, Ontario K1R 6P1
Canada
Tel: +1 613 233 1982
Fax: +1 613 233-9028
E-mail: pgs@web.apc.org
Website: http://www.web.apc.org/
~pgs/index.html

Abolition 2000: A Global Network to
  Eliminate Nuclear Weapons
c/o Nuclear Age Peace Foundation
1187 Coast Village Road, Suite 123
Santa Barbara, California 93108
United States
Tel: +1 805 965 3443
Fax: +1 805 568 0466
E-mail: wagingpeace@napf.org
Website: http://www.wagingpeace.org/
  abolition2000.html (with links to other
  Abolition 2000 websites)

Contributors

John Burroughs, the author, served as the World Court Project/IALANA legal coordinator at the November 1995 hearings before the International Court of Justice. He is an attorney for the Western States Legal Foundation, a non-profit group based in Oakland, California that monitors the U.S. nuclear weapon laboratories, and a member of the board of directors of the New York-based Lawyers' Committee on Nuclear Policy. *Nuclear Obligations*, his 1991 Ph.D. dissertation in the Jurisprudence & Social Policy Program, Boalt Hall School of Law, University of California at Berkeley, concerns the international law framework for nuclear weapon policy and protest. He also has a J.D. from Boalt Hall and a B.A. from Harvard.

Phon van den Biesen, who initiated and coordinated preparation of this book and contributed the foreword, since 1989 has been secretary of the International Association of Lawyers Against Nuclear Arms. He practices law in Amsterdam, and for many years has litigated nuclear and environmental issues on behalf of citizens' organizations in national and international courts. Since December 1993 he has acted as Deputy Agent of the Republic of Bosnia and Herzegovina before the International Court of Justice.

Recht und Zukunftsverantwortung
herausgegeben von Prof. Dr. jur. Alexander Roßnagel (Universität – Gesamthochschule Kassel)

Dieter Deiseroth
Berufsethische Verantwortung in der Forschung
Möglichkeiten und Grenzen des Rechts. Mit einem Geleitwort von Hans-Peter Dürr
Die vorliegende Studie widmet sich zwei Problemkreisen.
Zum einen geht sie der Frage nach, welche rechtlichen Spielräume Wissenschaftler und Ingenieure (beiderlei Geschlechts) im Bereich von Forschung und Entwicklung bei der Wahrnehmung ihrer berufsethischen Verantwortung nach geltendem Recht haben. Sind sie bei ihrer Tätigkeit wie andere Beschäftigte im Konfliktfalle letztlich dem Direktionsrecht des Arbeitgebers und den Weisungen der Vorgesetzten unterworfen oder können sie sich rechtlich mit Erfolg auf wissenschaftsspezifische Autonomiespielräume berufen?
Zweitens versucht sie die Frage zu beantworten, ob und gegebenenfalls welche rechtspolitischen Schritte sich zum Schutz und zur Förderung berufsethischer Verantwortung von Forscherinnen und Forschern empfehlen. Kann dabei auf den Erfahrungen mit US-amerikanischen Whistleblower-Schutzregelungen und Ethik-Codes aufgebaut werden?
Die Studie wendet sich nicht nur an die Angehörigen der juristischen Berufe, sondern gerade auch an Beschäftigte und Wissenschaftler in universitären und außeruniversitären Forschungseinrichtungen, Studenten sowie die interessierte Öffentlichkeit.
Bd. 1, 1997, 512 S., 48,80 DM, gb.,
ISBN 3–8258–3160–4

IALANA (Hrsg.)
Atomwaffen vor dem Internationalen Gerichtshof
Dokumentation – Analysen – Hintergründe.
Mit einem Geleitwort von Bundesverfassungsrichter a. D. DDr. Helmut Simon
Fast ein Jahrzehnt nach dem Ende des Kalten Krieges sind immer noch mehr als 20.000 nukleare Sprengkörper in den Arsenalen der Atomwaffenmächte einsatzfähig; weitere 20.000 Atomsprengköpfe liegen noch mehr oder weniger intakt bereit, weil der technische Prozeß der Abrüstung nur langsam vorankommt; gleichzeitig besteht die Gefahr der Weiterverbreitung (Proliferation) dieser Atomwaffen. Die vorhandenen Nuklearwaffen reichen aus, um unseren Planeten mehrfach zu zerstören. Solange Atomwaffen weiter existieren, ist die Gefahr der atomaren Vernichtung, und es sei "nur" aufgrund eines "menschlichen" oder "technischen Versagens", nicht gebannt.

Das am 8. Juli 1996 vom Internationalen Gerichtshof (IGH) in Den Haag verkündete Rechtsgutachten stellt einen Meilenstein in der Menschheitsgeschichte dar, mit Mitteln des Rechts zur Zivilisierung dieses Planeten beizutragen. Der vorliegende Band "ATOMWAFFEN VOR DEM INTERNATIONALEN GERICHTSHOF" dokumentiert diese bedeutsame und bisher öffentlich kaum beachtete IGH-Entscheidung, liefert Hintergrund-Informationen und lenkt den Blick auf die höchst praktischen Probleme einer Umsetzung des Richterspruchs.
"Wenn das Recht klar ist, gibt es eine größere Chance zur Einhaltung als wenn es in Unklarheit gehüllt ist." (IGH-Richter Weeramantry)
Bd. 2, 1997, 419 S., 29,90 DM, br.,
ISBN 3–8258–3243–0

Münsterische juristische Vorträge
herausgegeben von der Rechtswissenschaftlichen Fakultät der WWU Münster und der Juristischen Studiengesellschaft Münster

Hans Hattenhauer
Das heilige römische Reich und seine Staaten
Bd. 1, Herbst 1997, 64 S., 19,80 DM, br.,
ISBN 3–8258–3051–9

Münsteraner Einführungen: Rechtswissenschaft

Werner Krawietz
Grundprobleme des Rechts
Bd. 1, Herbst 1997, 130 S., 19,80 DM, br.,
ISBN 3–8258–2261–3

Werner Krawietz
Grundzüge der Rechtssoziologie
Bd. 2, Herbst 1997, 140 S., 29,80 DM, br.,
ISBN 3–8258–3144–2

Heinz Holzhauer
Deutsche Rechtsgeschichte
Bd. 4, Herbst 1997, 140 S., 19,80 DM, br.,
ISBN 3–8258–2262–1

Hans-Michael Wolffgang;
Michael Hendricks; Matthias Merz
Polizeirecht und allgemeines Ordnungsrecht Nordrhein-Westfalen
Das Polizei- und Ordnungsrecht nimmt einen herausgehobenen Platz in der Juristenausbildung ein. Es zählt zu den Kerngebieten des öffentlichen Rechts und ist regelmäßig Bestandteil der universitären Übungen und des juristischen Staatsexamens.

LIT Verlag Münster – Hamburg – London
Bestellungen über: Dieckstr. 73 48145 Münster Tel.: 0251 – 23 50 91 Fax: 0251 – 23 19 72

Der Band ist als Studienbuch konzipiert, das Lehrbuch, Fallsammlung und Schemata miteinander kombiniert. In der Studienliteratur zum Polizei- und Ordnungsrecht wird damit ein neuer Weg beschritten, der sich an den Bedürfnissen der Studierenden und den Anforderungen von Studium und Examen orientiert.
Zum Inhalt: Die Darstellung enthält die examensrelevanten Themen des Rechtsgebietes.
Der Lehrbuchteil ist eine an Struktur und Systematik orientierte Einführung und Vertiefung.
In der Fallsammlung werden die Sachverhalte gutachterlich bearbeitet und auf Examensniveau gelöst.
Strukturierte Übersichten und nützliche Prüfungsschemata dienen der schnellen Wiederholung.
Das Buch wendet sich an Studierende der Rechtswissenschaften. Es ist besonders für das Studium in Nordrhein-Westfalen geeignet, da es sich ausschließlich an der in diesem Bundesland geltenden Gesetzeslage orientiert.
Das Werk richtet sich an Studierende fortgeschrittener Semester, die bereits die Veranstaltungen zum Staatsrecht und zum Allgemeinen Verwaltungsrecht gehört haben.
Die Struktur entspricht der einer Fallsammlung, wobei die Fälle in erster Linie anhand aktueller Entscheidungen der Rechtsprechung dargestellt werden.
Zu allen Fällen werden Vertiefungshinweise auf die einschlägige Rechtsprechung und Literatur gegeben, die innerhalb der dargestellten Lösungswege an Streitpunkten dargestellt sind. Bei den Lösungen wurde drucktechnisch Platz für eigene Notizen gelassen. Dadurch soll sowohl ein Vorals auch das Nacharbeiten erleichtert werden.
Zusätzlich zu den "klassischen" Lösungsskizzen enthält das Werk eine Anzahl von Übersichten und Prüfungsschemata, die durch besondere Hervorhebungen innerhalb der einzelnen Lösungswege ergänzt werden, besondere Problemstrukturen hervorheben sowie Lernschwerpunkte setzen.
Hier schließt das Werk eine derzeit in der aktuellen Ausbildungsliteratur bestehende Lücke.
Für Examenskandidaten sollte dieses Werk aufgrund der hohen Klausurrelevanz dieses Rechtsgebietes von besonderem Interesse sein.
Bd. 5, 1997, 248 S., 34,80 DM, br.,
ISBN 3-8258-2929-4

Juristische Schriftenreihe

Frank Venjakob
Das Legalitätsprinzip im Grundbuchverfahren
Bd. 80, 1996, 192 S., 48,80 DM, gb.,
ISBN 3-8258-2839-5

Petra Popp
Ministerverantwortlichkeit und Ministeranklage im Spannungsfeld zwischen Verfassungsgebung und Verfassungswirklichkeit
Ein Beitrag zur Verfassungsgeschichte des Kurfürstentums Hessen
Bd. 81, 1996, 440 S., 68,80 DM, br.,
ISBN 3-8258-2847-6

Peter Steven Dickstein
Die Merkmale der Lebensversicherung im europäischen Binnenmarkt
Bd. 82, 1996, 320 S., 78,80 DM, br.,
ISBN 3-8258-2849-2

Staffan Wegdell
Die nationalen skandinavischen Straßengütertransportrechte und die Haftung des Spediteurs nach schwedischem, norwegischem, finnischem und dänischem Recht
Bd. 83, 1996, 296 S., 78,80 DM, br.,
ISBN 3-8258-2856-5

William H. Willms
Das Spannungsverhältnis von internationalem Wettbewerbs- und Vertragsrecht bei Ausnutzung eines Verbraucherschutzgefälles
Bd. 84, 1997, 320 S.; 88,80 DM, br.,
ISBN 3-8258-2888-3

Olaf Meinking
Kontrahierungszwang für private Fernsehveranstalter
Bd. 85, 1996, 136 S., 68,80 DM, br.,
ISBN 3-8258-2899-9

Kurt Zwingenberger
Die Europäische Konvention zum Schutz der Menschenrechte in ihrer Auswirkung auf die Bundesrepublik Deutschland
Der Verfasser hat dieses Thema von dem Heidelberger Verfassungs- und Verwaltungsrechtler Walter Jellinek 1955 erhalten.
Dem Hauptteil der Arbeit, der sich mit der Auslegung der Europäischen Menschenrechtskonvention und des sachlich entsprechenden deutschen Rechts beschäftigt, sind ein Abriß der geschichtlichen Entwicklung der Menschenrechte, eine Darstellung der Entstehung der Konvention und kurze Ausführungen philosophischer Art vorangestellt.
Der historische Abriß befaßt sich mit den geistesgeschichtlichen Hintergründen. Diesem folgt ein eingehender und gut dokumentierter Bericht der Entstehungsgeschichte der Menschenrechtskonvention (EMRK), die ohne die Bemühungen

LIT Verlag Münster – Hamburg – London
Bestellungen über: Dieckstr. 73 48145 Münster Tel.: 0251 – 23 50 91 Fax: 0251 – 23 19 72

der europäischen Bewegung und des Europarates 1948/49 wie der europäischen Regierungen der frühen fünfziger Jahre dieses Jahrhunderts nicht zu denken gewesen wäre. Der kurze philosophische Versuch verdeutlicht die naturrechtliche Position des Verfassers.

Der Hauptteil behandelt nacheinander die allgemeinen Probleme dieser Konvention: das parlamentarische Verfahren in der Bundesrepublik Deutschland, die Ratifikation, der personelle, sachliche, räumliche und zeitliche Geltungsbereich, die rechtliche Einordnung der EMRK in das Staats- und Völkerrecht der deutschen Bundesrepublik, das Verhältnis der einzelnen Tatbestände der EMRK zum deutschen Recht, das Rechtsschutzsystem und die Auslegung.

Der Kern der materiellen Tatbestände der EMRK wird dem deutschen Verfassungsrecht vorgeordnet, als Präzisierungen des Grundsatzes der Menschenrechte (Art. 1 GG) gedeutet und als gemäß Art. 79 Abs. 3 GG unabänderliche REchte angesehen.

Übereinstimmungen und Abweichungen zwischen dem deutschen Recht und den materiellen ARtikeln der EMRK sind ausführlich behandelt. Der Abschnitt VII: Inhalt der Konvention und des ersten Zusatzprotokolls als der erste ist Versuch einer Gesamtdarstellung der EMRK.
Bd. 87, Herbst 1997, 368 S., 78,80 DM, gb.,
ISBN 3-8258-2916-2

Wolfhart Nitsch
Die Haftungsverhältnisse in der bilanzrechtlichen Systematik unter besonderer Berücksichtigung der Rechnungslegungsvorschriften für Kreditinstitute
Bd. 88, 1996, 352 S., 78,80 DM, br.,
ISBN 3-8258-2952-9

Shyr-Hau Shyr
Die Konzentrationsbekämpfung durch Fusionskontrolle im Rundfunkbereich
Vergleich zwischen den Rechtssystemen in der Bundesrepublik Deutschland und in der Republik China (Taiwan)
Bd. 89, 1996, 216 S., 68,80 DM, br.,
ISBN 3-8258-2979-0

Andreas Wehlau
Die Rechtsprechung des Gerichtshofes der Europäischen Gemeinschaft zur Staatshaftung der Mitgliedstaaten nach Gemeinschaftsrecht
Ein Beitrag zur Funktion des Gerichtshofes im Rechtssystem der Gemeinschaft
Bd. 90, 1996, 168 S., 68,80 DM, br.,
ISBN 3-8258-3038-1

Jürgen W. Hidien
Ergänzungszuweisungen des Bundes gem. Art. 107 Abs. 2 Satz 3 des Grundgesetzes
Bd. 91, 1997, 328 S., 49,80 DM, br.,
ISBN 3-8258-3319-4

Anselm Brandi-Dohrn
Berechnung und heutige Berechtigung der Haftungssumme im internationalen Luftfrachttransport
Unter besonderer Berücksichtigung des Luftfrachtsammelladungsverkehrs
Bd. 92, 1997, 192 S., 88,80 DM, bf.,
ISBN 3-8258-3204-x

Nicola Gragert
Möglichkeiten und Grenzen der Flexibilisierung von Tarifverträgen zugunsten betrieblicher Regelungen
Bd. 93, Herbst 1997, 248 S., 68,80 DM, br.,
ISBN 3-8258-3337-2

Michael Preiß-Jankowski
Die gemeinschaftsrechtliche Staatshaftung im Lichte des Bonner Grundgesetzes und des Subsidiaritätsprinzips (Artikel 23 GG und Artikel 3b EGV)
Bd. 94, 1997, 296 S., 78,80 DM, br.,
ISBN 3-8258-3370-4

Jürgen Hidien
Die horizontale Steuerverteilung gem. Art. 107 Absatz 1 des Grundgesetzes
Bd. 95, 1997, 328 S., 58,80 DM, br.,
ISBN 3-8258-3475-1

Nils Thun
Die rechtsgeschichtliche Entwicklung des Stockwerkseigentums
Ein Beitrag zur deutschen Privatrechtsgeschichte
Bd. 96, Herbst 1997, 200 S., 69,80 DM, br.,
ISBN 3-8258-3493-x

Ulf Müller
Die rechtliche Stellung der Fachschaften
Bd. 97, 1997, 352 S., 59,80 DM, br.,
ISBN 3-8258-3502-2

Norbert Küper
Entlastung des Straßengüterverkehrs durch den Schienengüterverkehr
Historische, funktionale und rechtliche Aspekte
Bd. 98, Herbst 1997, 264 S., 48,80 DM, br.,
ISBN 3-8258-3579-0

LIT Verlag Münster – Hamburg – London
Bestellungen über: Dieckstr. 73 48145 Münster Tel.: 0251 – 23 50 91 Fax: 0251 – 23 19 72